The Beatles

AND THE SIXTIES

Michka Assayas
Claude Meunier

A Henry Holt Reference Book
Henry Holt and Company
New York

A PICTURE IS WORTH A THOUSAND WORDS

Xun Zi (313-238 B.C.)

A Henry Holt Reference Book
Henry Holt and Company, Inc.
Publishers since 1866
115 West 18th Street
New York, New York 10011

Henry Holt® is a registered trademark
of Henry Holt and Company, Inc.

Published in Canada by Fitzhenry & Whiteside Ltd.,
195 Allstate Parkway, Markham, Ontario L3R 4T8.

Library of Congress Cataloging-in-Publication Data
Assayas, Michka.
The Beatles and the sixties/Michka Assayas and Claude
Meunier.
p. cm.

—(W5 (who, what, where, when, and why) series)
Includes bibliographical references and index.
1. Beatles. 2. Rock musicians—England—Biography.
3. Rock music—1961-1970—History and criticism.
I. Meunier, Claude, 1948- . II. Title. III. Series.
ML421.B4A87 1996   96-26379
782.42166' 092' 2—dc20   CIP
                    [B]   MN

ISBN 0-8050-5059-0

Henry Holt books are available for special
promotions and premiums.
For details contact: Director, Special Markets.

Originally published in France in 1996 by
Editions Mango under the title *Les Beatles et les années 60*.

First published in the United States in 1996
by Henry Holt and Company, Inc.

First American Edition—1996
Idea and series by Dominique Gaussen
American English translation by Albert LaFarge
Typesetting by Jay Hyams and Christopher Hyams Hart

Printed in Italy by G. Canale & C. S.p.A. - Borgaro T.se - TURIN

All first editions are printed on acid-free paper. ∞

1 2 3 4 5 6 7 8 9 10

YOUR MOTHER SHOULD KNOW

In 1945, after more than five years of bitter fighting, World War II finally comes to a close. Old Europe is on its knees. Most of France's bridges and rail lines have been destroyed, and in Great Britain entire cities have been laid waste by bombing, among them Manchester and Liverpool. Germany lies in ruins: in the stores there is barely a safety pin left on the shelves, and the German mark has been devalued to virtually nothing—cigarettes are being used as the common currency. Throughout Europe, every basic commodity—coal for heating, electricity, meat—is subject to rationing. And such shortages continue to be felt through the 1940s. By the early 1960s, these conditions are memories, though still vivid, and for years to come the people of Europe will remain haunted by the horror of their recent history. Nonetheless, the Marshall Plan implemented by President Truman at the end of the war succeeds in restoring Europe to its prewar standard of living. To young Europeans struggling through the dreary grayness of the postwar recovery, the United States stands as a source of inspiration, with its convertible sports cars, its overnight millionaires, its adventure films shown in CinemaScope, its lighthearted sense of freedom and relaxation. America is the new El Dorado, where the biggest dreams can come true. In comparison, the countries of Europe seem almost backward. In France, for instance, those who can afford a new car in the early 1960s must wait a year or more for delivery; fewer than one household in ten has its own telephone; and only one in four has a record player. There is one television station, which sends out brief broadcasts at noon and again in the evening in black and white (color is still in the future); only about one household in eight has a television set. But the 1960s, the decade of the Beatles, brings unprecedented prosperity and consumption. While the dream of the New World was always tempered by the reality of Old Europe, the Beatles come to be seen as the bridge between the two.

LIVERPOOL:
ALL THE LONELY PEOPLE

On October 9, 1940, in a maternity ward on Oxford Street in Liverpool, the infant John Lennon lies in his crib beside his mother's bed. The bombs of the German Reich are falling around the city. Liverpool, a commercial port with a population of 700,000, is a strategic target in the war. Located on the west coast of England, just south of Wales and north of the Mersey River estuary, it is linked by canal to Manchester, northern England's industrial hub. Liverpool has seen prosperity in days past, when a bustling slave trade brought foreign wealth from abroad, until the practice was banned in the early nineteenth century. Later, the first great transatlantic merchant ships were built here. The cotton industry attracted many Irish laborers to Liverpool, including some of John Lennon's ancestors, as well as immigrants from France. With the decline of the cotton industry in the 1940s, Liverpool suffers an economic depression. The loss of foreign trade brings mass unemployment and poverty. The fathers of the Beatles are all of modest means, working at such jobs as ship's waiter (John's father), cotton salesman (Paul's), bus driver (George's), and baker (Ringo's). Their children grow up in a dreary, bombed-out city, isolated from the world and lacking in hopeful prospects for the future. A fatalistic and self-deprecating sense of humor takes hold among the Liverpudlians. Many of the city's young people dream of becoming actors or soccer players or famous musicians. In Liverpool, young and old alike find all sorts of occasions to get together and dance, sing, and make merry—at family get-togethers, at fairs, in pubs, at gatherings with fellow workers, on boats, at the skating rink, wherever. But with the sky hanging so low overhead, the boredom can be grinding, and the ocean invites journeys. Nowhere more than Liverpool does music represent an ideal way to blow off steam, and nowhere else does it offer such hope of a way out.

SKIFFLE

ROLL OVER BEETHOVEN

In the mid-1950s Liverpool's rock 'n' roll fans are in a sorry state. There seems to be no point in even dreaming of getting to see the likes of Chuck Berry, Bill Haley, or Carl Perkins live on stage—those American pioneers of rock 'n' roll can be heard only on the radio. In order to see live blues singers, a teenage Liverpudlian must hop aboard a bus for a ride to a theater in some distant suburb—only to hear no more than fifteen minutes of music crammed between juggling acts and other minor attractions. Naturally, the kids are overjoyed when Lonnie Donegan makes the scene at a local fish 'n' chips joint. This young Scotsman scratches out tunes on his banjo, imitating the sounds of the great New Orleans jazzmen. One evening during a break he grabs his banjo and starts belting out old American folk tunes—the young Brits are smitten with the sound. What they're hearing is something called "skiffle." This jazz term from the 1920s refers to the music of small Chicago bands who, lacking the money for real instruments, played whatever they could lay their hands on, like kazoos made out of a comb and paper, or broomstick basses, even washboards for percussion.

John Lennon, then 16 years old, comes down with a bad case of skiffle fever. He busts open his piggy bank to buy a 78-r.p.m. recording of "Rock Island Line" and practically wears it smooth before selling it to a chum. He pesters his Aunt Mimi until she finally breaks down and offers to buy him a guitar. In March 1957, young John and some school friends form a band called the Quarry Men Skiffle Group. They're not alone in their passion for skiffle music: at its peak, the skiffle craze spawns some 5,000 groups in England alone. The revolution is under way.

ROCK AND ROLL MUSIC

On November 15, 1956, the film *Love Me Tender* premières in New York City amid major hoopla. A 50-foot likeness of Elvis Presley is unveiled on the facade of the Paramount Theater. A few months later, in England, a throng of teenagers rush to Southampton to welcome one of rock 'n' roll's premier messengers, Bill Haley, whose hit "Rock Around the Clock" has come over from the New World to take the Old World by storm. When Haley arrives in London, a star-struck crowd gathers at the train station hoping to catch a glimpse of the star. Had it been Elvis, who knows what chaos would have broken loose—but Elvis doesn't tour outside the United States. With television still in its infancy, the only place for European fans to see the King of rock 'n' roll is the movie theater. Like their American counterparts, British teenagers go wild for this country boy who sings like an angel and dances like a man truly possessed. Elvis stares out at the audience with his James Dean-like expression of defiance mixed with melancholy. The hits "All Shook Up" and "Jailhouse Rock," both released in 1957, when Elvis was only 22 years old, electrify the United States and Europe. In Liverpool, as in other cities of the Old World, kids flock to theaters to see their favorite rock stars on screen. They also begin dreaming about a distant land where a young truck driver from Memphis could become an overnight sensation—and a millionaire. This is the American Dream, a Technicolor Oz where everything is simple and playful, a world where anything goes—in stark contrast to the gray and gloomy Europe where anything fun seems to be against the rules.

LIVERPOOL:

LIVERPOOL STADIUM
A boxing ring becomes the center stage for Liverpool's first major rock 'n' roll concert, on May 3, 1960, with Gene Vincent leading the bill. Among the warmup bands are Rory Storm and the Hurricanes and Gerry and the Pacemakers. The Silver Beatles, as they are then known, watch from the audience, since Allan Williams feels they are still too inexperienced to perform at the event.

LITHERLAND TOWN HALL, HATTON HILL ROAD, LITHERLAND
The popularity of the Beatles explodes here on December 27, 1960. At the instigation of disc-jockey Bob Wooler, they give a triumphant concert in this ballroom on their return from Hamburg. Liverpool has never seen so energetic a performance—or heard one so loud.

NEMS, 12-14 WHITECHAPEL
The record store run by Brian Epstein, who becomes the Beatles' manager in 1961.

TOWER BALLROOM, NEW BRIGHTON, WIRRAL
The great dancehall where, at the initiative of promoter Sam Leach, "Operation Big Beat" is organized at the end of 1961. More than 3,000 young fans show up to cheer their favorite local bands in a series of memorable evenings.

THE IRON DOOR CLUB, 13 TEMPLE STREET
Just steps away from the Cavern is another club where the leading "Mersey Beat" groups play all through the night of March 11, 1961, headed up by the Beatles. Among them are Rory Storm and the Hurricanes, the Big Three, the Searchers, the Remo Four, and Howie Casey and the Seniors.

THE CAVERN CLUB, 10 MATHEW STREET
The birthplace of the Beatles and the "Mersey Beat," the musical trend that rocked the whole area around the Mersey River estuary. Ray McFall, the Cavern's owner, has transformed an old jazz club into an amateur rock 'n' roll showcase. The reputation of the Beatles is closely linked with the Cavern, where they play innumerable concerts between 1961 and 1963. Gerry and the Pacemakers and the Searchers, to name just the most well-known bands, also get their start there, as do the Hollies and Freddie and the Dreamers, who come from the rival city of Manchester.

WYVERN SOCIAL CLUB, 108 SEEL STREET
The club where, on May 10, 1960, the Silver Beatles audition—unsuccessfully—to become the backup band accompanying the Liverpool rocker Billy Fury. Even so, they catch the attention of manager Larry Parnes.

PLACES TO REMEMBER

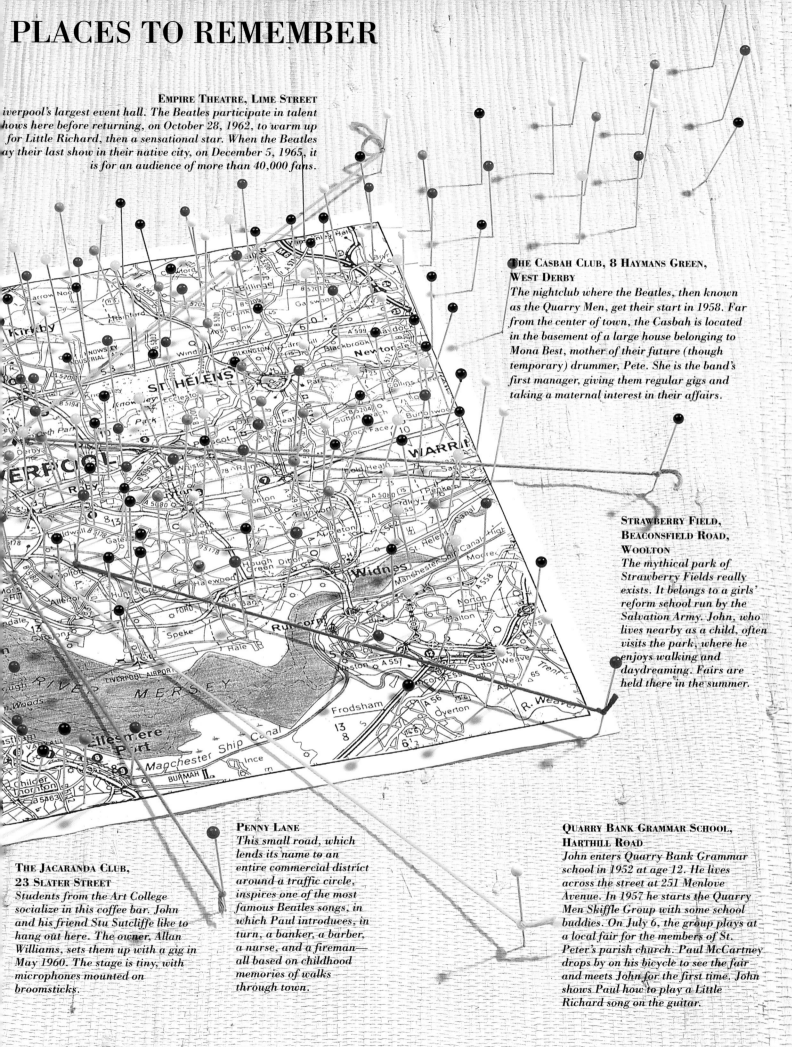

EMPIRE THEATRE, LIME STREET
*iverpool's largest event hall. The Beatles participate in talent
hows here before returning, on October 28, 1962, to warm up
for Little Richard, then a sensational star. When the Beatles
ay their last show in their native city, on December 5, 1965, it
is for an audience of more than 40,000 fans.*

**THE CASBAH CLUB, 8 HAYMANS GREEN,
WEST DERBY**
*The nightclub where the Beatles, then known
as the Quarry Men, get their start in 1958. Far
from the center of town, the Casbah is located
in the basement of a large house belonging to
Mona Best, mother of their future (though
temporary) drummer, Pete. She is the band's
first manager, giving them regular gigs and
taking a maternal interest in their affairs.*

**STRAWBERRY FIELD,
BEACONSFIELD ROAD,
WOOLTON**
*The mythical park of
Strawberry Fields really
exists. It belongs to a girls'
reform school run by the
Salvation Army. John, who
lives nearby as a child, often
visits the park, where he
enjoys walking and
daydreaming. Fairs are
held there in the summer.*

**THE JACARANDA CLUB,
23 SLATER STREET**
*Students from the Art College
socialize in this coffee bar. John
and his friend Stu Sutcliffe like to
hang out here. The owner, Allan
Williams, sets them up with a gig in
May 1960. The stage is tiny, with
microphones mounted on
broomsticks.*

PENNY LANE
*This small road, which
lends its name to an
entire commercial district
around a traffic circle,
inspires one of the most
famous Beatles songs, in
which Paul introduces, in
turn, a banker, a barber,
a nurse, and a fireman—
all based on childhood
memories of walks
through town.*

**QUARRY BANK GRAMMAR SCHOOL,
HARTHILL ROAD**
*John enters Quarry Bank Grammar
school in 1952 at age 12. He lives
across the street at 251 Menlove
Avenue. In 1957 he starts the Quarry
Men Skiffle Group with some school
buddies. On July 6, the group plays at
a local fair for the members of St.
Peter's parish church. Paul McCartney
drops by on his bicycle to see the fair
and meets John for the first time. John
shows Paul how to play a Little
Richard song on the guitar.*

BUDDY HOLLY AND THE CRICKETS
The first rock 'n' roll tune that John Lennon learns to play on the guitar is "That'll Be the Day," and it's also the first song that John, Paul, and George record together, with the help of pianist John Lowe and drummer Colin Hanton, neither of whom stay long with the band. The recording is made in Liverpool in 1958, in a small apartment transformed into a makeshift studio. Up to and even after his tragic death in 1959 at the age of 22, Buddy Holly and his band, the Crickets, are an inspiration to the future Beatles—and in more ways than just the reference to insects. The Texan crooner's rockabilly style, with his unique blend of tenderness and melodic subtlety, helps give the budding musicians the confidence to develop a musical style all their own.

THE QUARRY MEN
(March 1957-November 1959)
At age 16, John Lennon is armed with his mail-order guitar and is burning up with skiffle fever. He gets together with his buddies in March 1957 and forms the Quarry Men, a band named after their school. The kids play at local dives, sometimes even using the back of a pick-up truck as a stage. In July, Paul McCartney, then barely 15 years old, catches John's act at a local fair and is blown away by John's guitar-playing ability, especially his mastery of the songs of American rock star Little Richard. In February 1958, one of McCartney's friends, the 15-year-old George Harrison, who was an electrician's apprentice at the time, joins the band as backup guitarist, bringing the total number of members to seven. The other band members quit when John and his new friends start to move away from the skiffle sound as John, Paul, and George get more and more into rock 'n' roll. They are already trying out tunes like Chuck Berry's "Roll Over Beethoven," Gene Vincent's "Be-Bop-a-Lula," and Eddie Cochran's "Twenty Flight Rock," along with other American popular music, including adaptations of classic folk songs.

BEATLES
(August 1960-July 1961)
John makes the final decision in July 1960: henceforth, the band will be known as the Beatles, a compromise between "beat," as in rhythm, and "Beetles." With the help of a local entrepreneur named Allan Williams, who becomes their manager for a brief spell, the band lands a gig doing nightly shows at a club in Hamburg, Germany. Paul asks Pete Best, the son of the owners of the Casbah, to be the drummer for the Beatles, and the resulting quintet—John, Paul, George, Stu, and Pete—lasts a year. In the spring of 1961, after a second run of shows in Hamburg, Sutcliffe drops out of the band, preferring to remain in Hamburg with his new fiancée and pursue his painting. This is just after the band has made its first record, accompanying London singer Tony Sheridan on a rock version of "My Bonnie Lies Over the Ocean," which is released under the name of the Beat Brothers. Paul takes Sutcliffe's place as bass guitarist. Soon after, in April 1962, Sutcliffe dies tragically in Hamburg of a cerebral hemorrhage.

BEATLES
(August 1961-August 1962)
In early 1961, John, Paul, George, and Pete begin performing in Liverpool at the Cavern Club, where American celebrities like Little Richard and Gene Vincent also play. By this time the band is giving first-rate rock 'n' roll performances, and by the end of the year, Brian Epstein, a young record dealer, falls in with the group as their manager and promptly succeeds in arranging their first record company audition, at the Decca studios in London, in January 1962. But the executives at Decca are not impressed enough with the Beatles to offer them a record contract. Epstein and the Beatles get their revenge in June when George Martin, then a talent scout for EMI, signs the group to his label.

ORPHOSIS

JOHNNY & THE MOONDOGS
(November 1959-January 1960)

Beginning in 1959, John, Paul, and George seem to be approaching a deadend, with no gigs in sight. Finally, in August they get the Quarry Men back in action by landing an engagement at a place called the Casbah Coffee Club, accompanied by guitarist Ken Browne. When Browne leaves the band soon thereafter, they rename the resulting trio Johnny and the Moondogs, which has a very American ring to it. Though the name lasts only briefly, it is as Johnny and the Moondogs that John, Paul, and George play on stage for the first time outside Liverpool, at Manchester's Hippodrome Theatre, in a musical competition. (They have to leave before the finale.)

SILVER BEETLES
(January 1960-August 1960)

In January 1960, John Lennon signs up for classes at the Liverpool College of Art. There he meets Stu Sutcliffe, who already has an established reputation as a talented painter. At John's suggestion, Stu gets himself an electric bass guitar, but he never masters the instrument. Even so, Stu comes up with the name Beatals (after America's beatnik poets), later revising it to the Beetles, in memory of the late Buddy Holly and his band, the Crickets. The other band members are unsure about the name, but settle temporarily on the Silver Beetles. The band then lands a gig in Scotland backing-up an obscure Liverpool performer, Johnny Gentle, in May 1960. With them goes a 36-year-old factory worker named Tommy Moore, who joins the band briefly as drummer.

BEATLES
(August 1962-April 1970)

In August 1962, John, Paul, and George oust Pete Best from the band, mainly out of concern that his mother is meddling too much in their affairs. It is at this time that Ringo Starr quits his job as drummer for another Liverpool rock group, Rory Storm and the Hurricanes, to replace Best. John, Paul, George, and Ringo are now united—and destined for eternal fame as the Fab Four.

"If you remember the sixties, then you must have missed them." Or so goes the saying. For the most adventurous—or perhaps the most reckless—the sixties are nothing less than a nonstop party. And the joy-makers wake up with a wicked hangover the morning after. The wild decade of the Beatles sees the rise of the miniskirt, an explosion of psychedelic colors, the loosening of morality, and the blossoming of hedonistic pleasure. There is an optimistic attitude that the world is a good place and everything will turn out okay; young people especially have a willingness to trust in the future that seems impossibly naive by today's standards. But even among young people there are differences, especially between Americans and Europeans. In the United States, where rock and roll first burst on the scene in the 1950s, kids are well ahead of their European counterparts and have already begun to create a world of their own. They are experiencing things that are still unthinkable in Europe. At high schools across America, boys are allowed to wear blue

DRIVE MY CAR

jeans, and girls wear tight skirts. They can chew gum and drink soda. Kids from middle-class families are allowed to borrow their parents' car, and the wealthiest kids are given cars of their own—maybe even a convertible. All this is envied by kids in Europe, where life just isn't the same. In England, schoolchildren have no styles they can be proud of. They have to wear uniforms and obey the strict discipline of the headmaster, who has the right to inflict corporal punishment on errant students. In France, young students have to wear smocks at school, blue for boys and pink for girls. Even high school students are closely monitored, and the threat of Saturday detention hangs over them. In the United States, the latest pop hits can be heard on the radio or juke boxes. In France, all you can get on the radio is traditional French music; to hear the newest music from other countries, you have to listen to versions made by French singers. For the majority of young French people, the party is still off-limits, the stuff of dreams.

DECEMBER 31, 1962

"Love Me Do" comes out at the end of 1962.
What's going on in the world at the time?

May 8, 1945: The German army surrenders. The armistice signed at Rheims officially ends World War II in Europe.

July 1945: The Potsdam Conference determines the fate of postwar Germany. Americans take the Rhineland and south, British forces occupy the north, and the Soviets take the east.

August 6, 1945: An American airplane drops the first atomic bomb on Hiroshima, Japan, killing 100,000 citizens. Three days later, another bomb is exploded over Nagasaki. The Japanese surrender.

October 1, 1946: The military tribunal at Nuremberg condemns 11 Nazi officials to death by hanging.

1947: George C. Marshall, Truman's secretary of state, engineers the "plan" that bears his name. The United States agrees to aid Europe in rebuilding, under the condition that America install military bases as a buffer against the Soviet Union. The cold war has begun.

August 15, 1947: India gains its independence and ceases to be a British colony.

January 30, 1948: Mahatma Gandhi, apostle of nonviolence, is assassinated.

May 14, 1948: David Ben-Gurion proclaims the independence of Israel. War immediately follows with the neighboring Arabs. Israel emerges the victor in 1949, marking the beginning of a protracted anti-Israeli guerrilla war.

February-March 1949: An American Boeing B-50 achieves the first uninterrupted flight around the world after 45 hours in the air.

October 1, 1949: In China, Communist leader Mao Zedong proclaims the birth of the People's Republic of China.

June 25, 1950: North Korean forces invade South Korea beginning the Korean War (1950-53). American and U.N. forces under General Douglas MacArthur drive the North Korean Communist forces back to the border with China. When the North Koreans attack again, MacArthur wants to declare all-out war, but President Truman removes him from command (1951).

February 6, 1952: In Great Britain, Elizabeth II succeeds George VI.

March 1953: The Soviet dictator Stalin dies at age 74; Nikita Khrushchev gradually assumes the reins of power.

May 1954: In Vietnam, the occupying French are defeated at Dien Bien Phu by the troops of Ho Chi Minh. France abandons the country, which is subsequently divided into the North, supported by Communist China, and the South, supported by the United States.

May 17, 1954: In the United States, the Supreme Court rules that racial segregation in schools is unconstitutional.

November 1954: In Algeria, armed militants launch attacks on the French colonial authorities. France sends in troops.

February 1956: At the 20th Congress of the Communist Party in the Soviet Union, Khrushchev delivers an official indictment of Stalin.

July 1956: Egyptian President Nasser decides to nationalize the Suez Canal. England and France attempt to send a flotilla to defend their interests, but are restrained by America and the Soviet Union.

October 1956: In a bloody encounter in Budapest, Hungary, Soviet tanks are deployed to suppress a popular anticommunist uprising.

October-November 1956: Israel attacks Egypt, conquering the Sinai desert.

1957: Popular demonstrations increase in European capital cities against the use of the atomic bomb.

August 28, 1957: The U.S. Congress passes the Civil Rights Act of 1957, empowering the Justice Department to go to court in cases where blacks are denied the right to vote. The period of the civil rights movement is now launched.

November 3, 1957: The Soviet Union launches the *Sputnik II* satellite bearing the dog Laika, which becomes the first living creature sent into space.

January 1959: In Cuba, Fulgenico Batista's forces are routed by anti-American guerrilla forces led by Fidel Castro.

October 4, 1959: The Soviet space rocket *Lunik III* transmits the first images of the dark side of the moon.

1960: The end of the great European empires in Africa: Belgium cedes independence to the Congo, and France gives up all its old colonies in Africa, followed soon after by Great Britain.

1960: In the United States, John F. Kennedy, a 43-year-old Democrat and Catholic, is elected president.

Summer 1960: At the Olympics in Rome, the Soviet Union brings home 84 gold medals, more than any other nation.

April 12, 1961: Soviet cosmonaut Yuri Gagarin is the first human to circle the Earth in space, aboard the *Vostok I*.

April 17, 1961: Failure of the American landing at the Bay of Pigs in Cuba. Castro agrees to exchange American prisoners for medical supplies.

May 1961: The head of the University of Mississippi bars entry to the school's first black student, James Meredith, prompting police intervention.

August 1961: In an attempt to stem the tide of human and economic resources from East Germany, the Soviet-backed government decides to erect a thirty-mile wall in Berlin patrolled by 10,000 guards.

February 20, 1962: American astronaut John Glenn circles the Earth three times in the rocket *Friendship VIII*, launched as part of the Mercury space program.

March 1962: At a meeting in Evian, France signs an accord granting independence to Algeria.

October 1962: The United State organizes a naval blockade of Cuba to prevent Soviet ships from installing missile-launching pads there. The confrontation, known as the Cuban missile crisis, ends with the removal of the Soviet weapons.

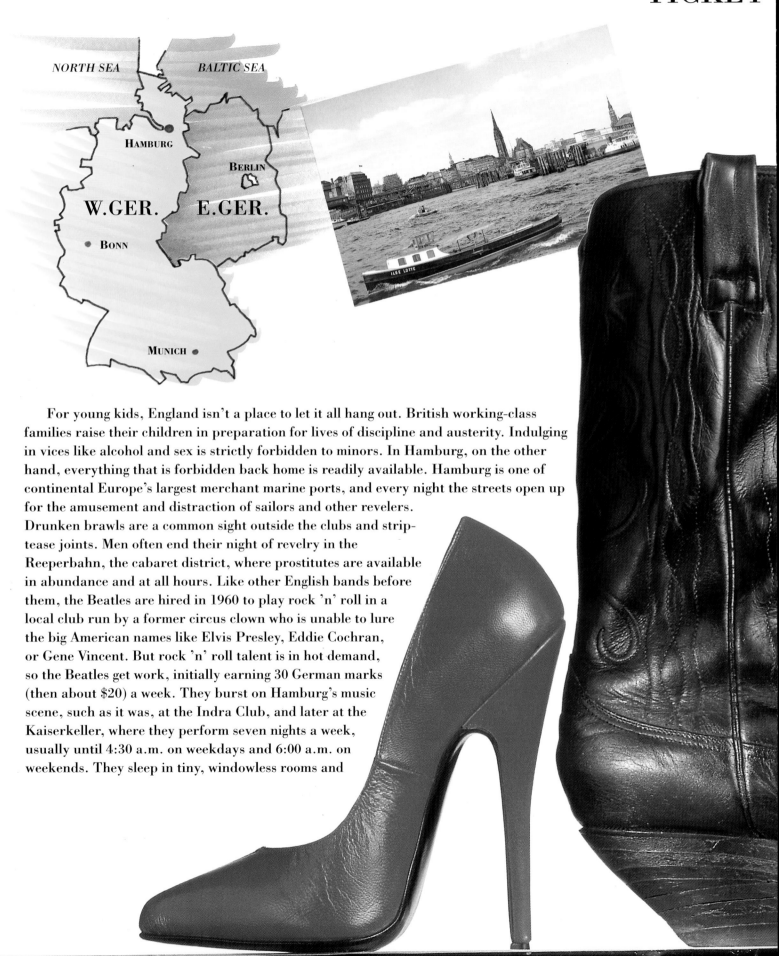

NORTH SEA

BALTIC SEA

HAMBURG

BERLIN

W.GER.

E.GER.

BONN

MUNICH

ILSE LOTTE

For young kids, England isn't a place to let it all hang out. British working-class families raise their children in preparation for lives of discipline and austerity. Indulging in vices like alcohol and sex is strictly forbidden to minors. In Hamburg, on the other hand, everything that is forbidden back home is readily available. Hamburg is one of continental Europe's largest merchant marine ports, and every night the streets open up for the amusement and distraction of sailors and other revelers. Drunken brawls are a common sight outside the clubs and strip-tease joints. Men often end their night of revelry in the Reeperbahn, the cabaret district, where prostitutes are available in abundance and at all hours. Like other English bands before them, the Beatles are hired in 1960 to play rock 'n' roll in a local club run by a former circus clown who is unable to lure the big American names like Elvis Presley, Eddie Cochran, or Gene Vincent. But rock 'n' roll talent is in hot demand, so the Beatles get work, initially earning 30 German marks (then about $20) a week. They burst on Hamburg's music scene, such as it was, at the Indra Club, and later at the Kaiserkeller, where they perform seven nights a week, usually until 4:30 a.m. on weekdays and 6:00 a.m. on weekends. They sleep in tiny, windowless rooms and

TO RIDE

make do with water from the urinal for washing. To keep them going all night, the band members drink beer and coffee during their gigs, in addition to popping amphetamines supplied by the cleaning lady. It is in Hamburg that the group picks up their first leather rocker outfits, have loads of wild times with the local girls, and start getting into trouble with the local street ruffians. But at the same time, the band is evolving musically into a rock ensemble of exceptional energy and enthusiasm.

Beyond their successful adaptations of American rhythm and blues standards and rock 'n' roll hits, the Beatles begin writing their own material. Between 1960 and 1962 the band spends a total of about four months in Hamburg, finishing with runs at their most fashionable venues to date, the Top Ten and the Star Club. The trial by fire that was Hamburg has polished their skills, burnished their natural talents, and not the least steeled them for the battle ahead—in which they will conquer the world.

BEFORE EPSTEIN

WITH

Late in 1961, young people begin showing up at the NEMS store in Liverpool asking for a certain record originally released in Germany: the song is called "My Bonnie," and the artist is Tony Sheridan, accompanied by the Beat Brothers, better known locally as the Beatles. The store's proprietor, Brian Epstein, has never heard of the record, but his curiosity is piqued. He soon discovers that a local magazine called *Mersey Beat*, which young people buy at his store, lists the Beatles as the most popular band in town. As it happens, Epstein's store is located in the Whitechapel area of town, just steps away from the Cavern Club, where the Beatles are playing a regular lunch-hour show. Epstein decides to drop by and check out the band for himself. He is dazzled by what he hears. Brian Epstein is 27 years old and comes from a respectable family of Jewish merchants; his tastes run to jazz and classical music. In fact, he has always harbored a dream of becoming a stage actor, but as fate would have it, he winds up pursuing a different dream when early

in 1962 he prevails upon the Beatles to let him act as their manager. Before Epstein enters their lives, the Beatles resemble nothing more than a bunch of street punks in leather outfits, cursing onstage, chomping on chicken wings between sets, and joking idly with the audience. Epstein is not impressed with any of this, and he quickly puts an end to their smoking, drinking, and gum chewing during performances. He also cuts out the small talk with the audience. From now on, the Beatles will be the tightest act in town and will conduct themselves in a strictly businesslike manner. Their greased-back hair yields to a new mop-top style that is the newest fashion in Paris. The leather outfits are replaced with collarless mohair jackets and ties, with matching pants, also brought in from Paris. In order to capture and seduce a large audience, the Beatles themselves need to be tamed, and under Epstein's management, rigorous discipline is the order of the day. Hence forward, the strategy will be to trade shock value for mass appeal, and the payback comes soon enough in the form of worldwide success.

WE LOVE YOU, YEAH, YEAH, YEAH...

By the end of the 1950s, many adults think rock 'n' roll threatens to bring riots and destruction in its wake. In England as elsewhere, newspapers, radio, and other mouthpieces of the older generation come down full force against this "degenerate" new music. In France, President Charles de Gaulle goes so far as to suggest that unruly teenagers direct their boundless energy to productive ends, such as road building, instead of screaming at rock concerts. But within a few years, the situation changes. By the early 1960s, the frustrating effects of wartime rationing have finally begun to recede in England, and the Marshall Plan is credited with achieving its intended effects in Europe as a whole. The well-fed youth population glows with optimism about the future, and their screams are now recognized as expressions of enthusiasm and joy rather than violence and anguish. On October 13, 1963, a crowd of young people gathers in front of a London theater where the Beatles are recording a televised concert for broadcast all across the country. Most of the screaming comes from girls and young women, who stomp their feet and even cry because they might not get a chance to touch one of the Fab Four. The police do their best to clear out the area, but the ecstatic mob has a will of its own. One song in particular, floating out from the soundstage, ignites an explosion of hysterical cries: "From Me to You," with its high voices sung in unison against an insistent backbeat. During the final tune, "She Loves You," the entire crowd joins in the chorus, filling the streets of London with the jubilant refrain: "Yeah, yeah, yeah!" The energy is overwhelming, and all of it is innocent fun. London's *Daily Mirror* hails the frenzy of enthusiasm, coining the term *Beatlemania* to describe the atmosphere of the evening. Two months later, the four Beatles are invited to perform at a gala event attended by Queen Elizabeth herself, along with her daughter, the young Princess Margaret. On that evening, the ever-iconoclastic John Lennon delivers this legendary remark to the audience: "Will people in the cheaper seats clap your hands? All the rest of you, if you'll just rattle your jewelry."

1964:
YOU'VE GOT THAT SOMETHING

On February 7, 1964, a crowd of star-struck teenagers gathers at New York City's John F. Kennedy Airport to welcome the Beatles to the New World—a spectacular reversal of the reception that had greeted Bill Haley in London seven years earlier. "I Want to Hold Your Hand" is at the top of the American charts, and the Fab Four's arrival in New York inaugurates two weeks of hysteria. "Beatlemania" has arrived from Jolly Old England and spreads across the New World like wildfire. A throng of 60,000 screaming fans begs in vain for a seat in the CBS television studio where the Beatles are scheduled to appear on the "Ed Sullivan Show." Some 6,000 people succeed in making their way in, finding standing room where possible among the studio's 700 seats. It is a scene of total mayhem. The "British Invasion" has begun, and the boys from Liverpool are seen and heard everywhere in the United States. The young of America, who have so recently discovered Elvis Presley and his wild gyrations, are now completely under the spell of the Beatles. Things are changing in America, to be sure. Since Elvis's national appearances in 1956, demonstrations for civil rights for black people, the assassination of President Kennedy, and the growing entanglement of American troops in Vietnam have all contributed to a climate of confusion and skepticism. The Beatles, with their youthful enthusiasm, come as a refreshing antidote to America's self-doubt. These young, working-class British lads seem to have no doubts about America's claim to greatness, and their songs cheerfully proclaim a naive belief in the American Dream. Artfully combining the best of American musical influences—the vocal style of black rhythm-and-blues groups from the 1950s, the primitive excitement of rock 'n' roll, the flair of Elvis, and the slickness of the American "hit parade"—the Beatles have learned from the Yanks and can now beat them at their own game. And even if certain curmudgeonly critics deride their mod hairstyles, no one can deny that the Beatles are hot. They are a *phenomenon*, and everyone wants to know what they're up to.

"I LOVE JOHN"

"I LOVE PAUL"

"I LOVE GEORGE"

"I LOVE RINGO"

ON THE ROAD

WITH THE BEATLES

"The show lasts twenty minutes, and nobody's listening, they're just screaming, and the amps are as big as peanuts." There is little nostalgia in John Lennon's recollection of playing with the Beatles in concert. After a brief visit to the United States in February 1964, the band embarks on an ambitious world tour, beginning with stints in the former British colonies of Australia and New Zealand. They return to America at the end of the summer for a month-long series of concerts scheduled to coincide with the release of their new movie, *A Hard Day's Night*, and the accompanying album soundtrack. The Beatles make history by becoming the first band to fill entire stadiums with tens of thousands of shrieking fans. There is hardly an arena big enough to accommodate these mega-concerts. Sound engineers struggle to cobble together public-address systems big enough to fill the amphitheaters with sound, but the equipment frequently proves inadequate. To make matters worse, the musicians don't have stage monitors and are thus unable to hear their voices or instruments during performances. And the uninterrupted shrieking of thousands of hysterical fans achieves a decibel level that, according to George Martin,

who is at the mixing board, makes it impossible to hear a jet plane flying directly overhead. The adoration is so extreme that police officers are dispatched to protect the musicians from their fans. On August 15, 1965, while on tour to promote the movie and album entitled *Help!* the Beatles set a new record for concert attendance when 55,600 people turn out to see them at New York's Shea Stadium. But these monster tours end the next year. The band becomes increasingly discouraged by mega-concerts in which the music itself seems to count for so little. As a result, the Beatles decide that they will abandon the stage for good after their concert at Candlestick Park in San Francisco on August 29, 1966, which is the last stop on that tour. From that point on, they remain cloistered in the privacy of the recording studio and devote themselves more than ever to writing and recording new material. Their last public appearance is an impromptu concert on January 30, 1969, atop the Abbey Road building, where their studio is housed, an event that becomes part of the documentary film *Let It Be*. Years later, in 1976, asked to describe his version of paradise, John Lennon responds flatly, "Not going on the road."

WE'RE MORE POPULAR

Widespread though it is, enthusiasm for the Beatles is not universal. When they land for the first time in the United States, in February 1964, the Beatles face a campaign called "Stop the Beatles!" spearheaded by a law student with a crew-cut who is horrified by their hairstyles. Even the King himself, Elvis Presley, despite having received the Beatles amicably enough as his guest at his Bel Air mansion in August 1965, is said to have written the F.B.I. voicing his concern about the danger the band poses in encouraging America's young people to go soft and effeminate. In the eyes of many conservatives, including some young people, the Beatles are the embodiment of all that is detestable: rebellion against authority, physical and "moral" permissiveness, and a surrender to baser instincts. In the United States, hostility toward the Beatles quickly turns into a powerful, well-organized

THAN JESUS NOW

campaign. In February 1966, during an interview for the British daily newspaper *The Evening Standard*, John replies to a journalist's question with a laugh and an offhand remark: "We're more popular than Jesus now." Months later, the American magazine *Datebook* reprints the interview and blows John's remark out of all proportion. The words echo throughout the media, letting loose the wrath of America's conservative population, who have suspected all along that behind the Beatles' madcap facade lurk the messengers of Satan. In Birmingham, Alabama, a group of citizens organize a mass protest, heaping Beatles records and posters onto a giant bonfire—an event blessed by local representatives of the Ku Klux Klan. By the time the Beatles touch down in Chicago, it has become clear that their concert tour cannot get underway until John, with his fellow Beatles at his side, faces the television cameras and offers a public apology for his supposedly sacrilegious remark. But even this is not enough to appease their enemies; the band members continue to receive death threats throughout the tour. They give their last performances in fear, haunted by the thought of a deranged assassin lurching out from the crowd at any moment, pistol in hand.

WHO'S MEANER, MR. MUSTARD

Under Brian Epstein's guidance, the Beatles become known as four well-behaved, happy-go-lucky boys whom any mother would gladly invite over for tea. Ironically, it is a former employee of Epstein's, Andrew Loog Oldham, who encourages five well-bred kids from London's south end to adopt all of the nasty habits the Beatles left behind in Hamburg. These are the Rolling Stones, who cultivate the look of rebellious street kids—rough around the edges, and generally antagonistic to the established order of things. The contrast with the Beatles is stark, and the press makes a big deal of it. The Beatles come across as humble, naive, and sentimental, with a penchant for colorful fantasies, even if occasionally a tad arrogant. But they recoil from any expression of violence or provocation. The Stones, as they come to be known, are contemptuous of all that is sentimental and sweet in popular music and instead cultivate a harsher, more confrontational style designed to provoke the rage of average God-fearing Britons, especially the parents of young children. Their public message is summed up by the title of one of their hits: "Paint It Black."

OR JUMPIN' JACK FLASH?

Backstage the story is slightly different. While there is surely some jealously, especially on John's part, in having to sit back and watch the Stones get to play the bad boys, their commercial rivalry is largely mythical. In reality, their managers find it more effective to cooperate than compete, and the result is a carefully orchestrated sharing of the market, with singles timed for release in alternate months to avoid direct conflicts on the pop charts. Among the band members themselves, there is friendship and mutual admiration. John and Paul first hear the Stones in 1963, at their London debut, and are so impressed with what they see that they offer the Stones an unpublished song, "I Want to Be Your Man," to use on their second single. Later, the Stones invite John and Paul to sing backup for the chorus on "We Love You" in 1967. John also takes part in the Stones' televised special *Rock 'n' Roll Circus* the next year. Brian Jones and Keith Richards often drop in on the Beatles during recording sessions. In the drama of the 1960s, there are heroes and there are villains. The Beatles and the Stones artfully divide those roles.

THE YOUTH MOVEMENT:
TWIST AND SHOUT

Before the 1960s, young people were expected to do nothing
but prepare to get old. They dressed like their parents, learned to speak like
them, and were generally expected to follow in their footsteps.
When a kid asked for something that wasn't part of the program,
some parent was sure to say, "We'll see when you get older." Around the middle
of the 1960s, this begins to change as the "baby boom" of the late 1940s begins
to take effect. More people are teenagers than ever before:
they're everywhere, and since their parents have more money than before,
the teenagers have it too. They form an entire new market unto themselves
and begin filling their rooms with records (45-r.p.m. singles
in the early days), comic books, magazines, and posters.
For the first time in recorded history, a kid's room is a private place within the
household: parents are banned (Do Not Enter: even to clean up!).

With the new postwar prosperity, parents find themselves able to give their
children transistor radios, record players, even guitars.

All over the U.S. and western Europe, clothing stores open up in the
bigger cities with products designed to meet the new demands, allowing
adolescents to find their own favorite fashions. And they wear them proudly:
blue jeans, jackets, and suede shoes for boys, and before long, short skirts and
bright blouses for girls. At first, only the most cosmopolitan of city dwellers can
benefit from this new freedom; most girls still have to make do with
what Mom brings home from the department store. And besides,
drab dress codes are still in force in many places (even wearing makeup is
against the rules). But the genie is out of the bottle, and young people become a
permanent part of the economic marketplace, ever more appealing
as a commercial target. Their styles, language, habits, indeed their whole
outlook on life take on an unprecedented importance in the larger society.

FOUR MAGICIANS

66 That night, I dreamed about the Beatles. My brother was hiding in the woods, and I took off to look for him, accompanied by Paul and John, who were running in the grass alongside me. At school, when I'm bored, I stare out the window and imagine that Paul has appeared outside, invisible to everybody but me. Sunday afternoon, at home, when everyone has gone off on their own, I hole up in the closet with the liner notes to *Magical Mystery Tour* and try to learn the lyrics to 'I

Am the Walrus' by heart. I sing as quietly as I can, fearing that someone might overhear me and make fun of me. I try to imitate John's nasal singing voice on that song, I'm crazy about it, even though I'm a bit unsure what the lyrics mean. 'I am he as you are he as you are me and we are all together' or 'Sitting on a cornflake, waiting for the van to come' or 'GOO GOO JOOB'— how does he do it? I try to get the lyrics down. I close the album cover and recite what I've learned so far. It's so

IN MY ROOM

much fun. I love how they keep repeating 'ho ho ha ha' at the end, louder and louder. My dad must think they're completely nuts. Mom actually likes the Beatles a lot. She bought us a copy of the single 'All You Need Is Love,' and we played it about a hundred times on the record player in her bedroom. Mom loves the way Paul sings 'Yesterday.' She's right; it's pretty. I have to admit though, I laugh at her behind her back because she doesn't know about all the drug references in 'A Day in the Life,' to LSD and everything. My brother told me about them. I pasted a picture of Paul's face in my science book at the page with the anatomy lesson: imagine the face my teacher would make if he saw it! It would be cool if John and Paul could come to my school. We'd forget about the rain and being bored in class—they would be like those magicians dressed in Technicolor outfits who can make everything disappear. "

GEORGE MARTIN: MUSICAL MENTOR

From 1962 to 1970, all of the Beatles recordings are made at the Abbey Road studios in London, under the supervision of George Martin. Far more than a mere technician, Martin takes on the role of mentor and father figure to the Beatles. This 35-year-old former Royal Air Force lieutenant comes from modest origins but has received classical training in piano and oboe. His schedule includes a monthly job conducting a local school orchestra. Beneath a slightly starchy exterior reminiscent of a friendly village pastor, Martin conceals a whimsical artistic temperament that blossoms in contact with the Beatles. It is Martin who first discovers the band on behalf of EMI records, where he was running a small division called Parlophone, devoted mainly to light music of the kind one might hear on British variety shows. The band's first audition, in May 1962, makes little impression on Martin, and he initially plans to set them up as a backup band for an artist who sang in the style of Cliff Richard, but on hearing the tune "Please Please Me" Martin completely changes his mind about the band's potential. Until 1965, Martin is satisfied with ensuring merely that the band's instruments are in tune, that the harmonies are right, and that the rhythm is solid. Then one morning Paul McCartney wakes up humming a ballad that has come to him out of the blue. When Martin hears Paul's rendition of "Yesterday," he's inspired to set the tune's guitar and vocal parts to the accompaniment of a string quartet and immediately sets to work on the parts. Martin's musical contributions steadily grow, and as the Beatles begin to invent increasingly fanciful and complicated arrangements, Martin lends his encouragement and expertise in realizing their musical ideas. For "Tomorrow Never Knows," a song released on the *Revolver* album, John wants his voice to sound "as though I'm the Dalai Lama chanting from the highest mountaintop." To achieve this, Martin comes up with the idea of adding just a touch of distortion to John's voice by running the signal through the revolving speaker in a Hammond organ. In addition, he takes a vocal track of Paul laughing and runs it at high speed, creating a weird noise that emulates the sound of seagulls. At Paul's suggestion, Martin adds a Bach trumpet line as ornament to "Penny Lane"; he also writes an arrangement of trumpets and cello parts for "Strawberry Fields Forever." Martin displays unprecedented creativity in his approach to multitrack recording, modifying the speed, tonal qualities, and even direction of individual tracks to suit the occasion. And the results are truly remarkable. His technical contributions climax in the recording of *Sergeant Pepper's Lonely Hearts Club Band*. Beyond hiring a full orchestra and chorus, he proceeds to stack layer upon layer of vocal tracks and inserts a variety of odd noises, modulating them at will to create hallucinatory effects, most notably in the celebrated "A Day in the Life." George Martin's innovations put recording engineers on the map as serious artists in their own right, particularly in the context of the new phenomenon of the "rock album," in which an album is more than just a collection of singles.

Drug use spreads far and wide during the 1960s. Mirroring their era, the Beatles try them all, for better or for worse. "I think the basic thing nobody asks is why do people take drugs of any sort? And that question has to be resolved before you can think, well, what can we do for the poor drug addict? Why do we have to have these accessories to normal living to live? I mean, is there something wrong with society that's making us so pressurized, that we cannot live without guarding ourselves against it? . . . You need hope, and hope is something that you build up within yourself and with your friends. It's a very difficult situation, drugs. . . . The worst drugs are as bad as anybody's told you. It's just a dumb trip, which I can't condemn people if they get into it, because one gets into it for one's own personal, social, emotional reasons. It's something to be avoided if one can help it."
John, press conference, December 21, 1969

DRUGS: FOR BETTER

"Those who think this a low-down dirty thing to smoke pot will be further convinced they're right and we're wrong. But it will strengthen the others who follow us. We were once everybody's darlings. But it isn't like that anymore. They hate us."
George, March 31, 1969, after being arrested for possession of marijuana on the day of Paul and Linda's wedding. John had paid a fine in November 1968 for the same offense.

"Up until LSD, I never realized that there was anything beyond this state of consciousness. The first time I took it, it just blew everything away. I had such an incredible feeling, that there was a God and I could see him in every blade of grass. It was like gaining hundreds of years' experience within twelve hours. It changed me and there was no way back to what I was before. It wasn't all good because it left a lot of questions as well."
George, 1987.

"I've always needed a drug to survive. The others, too, but I always had more. I always took more pills, more of everything because I'm crazy probably."
John, 1970.

"Heroin? It wasn't too much fun. I never injected or anything. Yoko and I sniffed a little when we were in real pain. I mean we just couldn't. . . . People were giving us such a hard time." John, 1970. His heroin habit lasts more than a year, from 1968 to 1970.

"If you find yourself at the edge of a cliff and you wonder whether you should jump or not— try jumping."
John, end of the 1960s.

"I was the first one on coke, which horrified the whole group. The minute I stopped, the whole record industry has got into it and never has stopped since."
Paul, 1986.

AND FOR WORSE

"Linda and me came over for dinner once and John said, 'You fancy getting the trepanning thing done?' I said, 'Well, what is it?' and he said, 'Well, you kind of have a hole bored into your skull and it relieves the pressure.' Now this wasn't a joke, this was like, Let's go next week, we know a guy who can do it and maybe we can do it all together. So I said, 'Look, you go and have it done, and if it works, great. Tell us about it and we'll have it.' John was more open to that kind of things." Paul, 1986, recounting memories from the years 1969-70.

A revolution rocks the West Coast of the United
States in the mid-1960s. At the vanguard is Timothy
Leary (1920-96), a researcher in the psychology department
at Harvard University. While traveling in California, Leary
experiments with peyote, a form of cactus plant with
hallucinogenic properties. It's a revelation for him: the drug
is capable of breaking the chains that normally control human
consciousness. Following the example of Aldous Huxley, the
British author of *Brave New World* and *The Doors of
Perception*, Leary becomes fascinated by a chemical
derivative of lysergic diethylamide acid known as LSD 25.
This hallucinogenic drug is capable of altering a person's
perception of the world, bringing into view a whole new
universe of forms and colors that defy description to the
uninitiated. Above all, the mysterious substance seems to lift
the user into a superior state of consciousness approaching
religious revelation. After being dismissed from Harvard,
Leary publishes his findings in a new magazine called *The
Psychedelic Review*. A word is coined to describe an era; in
California, "psychedelic" experimentation spreads like
wildfire, and LSD becomes the drug of choice, especially
among young musicians. At the famous Stanford
University, in Palo Alto just south of San Francisco,
a group of students participates in a government
program to test the effects of the new drug. Among
these students is writer Ken Kesey, whose crusading
enthusiasm leads to the formation of his band of
Merry Pranksters. Together they organize the first
"Acid Tests," with participants all taking the drug
together. These parties often culminate in wild
excursions in the Pranksters' brightly decorated
bus. Many bands from the San Francisco area fall
in with the Pranksters, most notably the band
the Grateful Dead. LSD is outlawed in 1966,
but by that time it has taken root as the source
of a new phenomenon, known as "psychedelic
music," after its usefulness in exploring the
psyche. The phrase doesn't apply to any
particular style of music so much as to a whole
new musical approach—unrestrained and unruly,
free of traditional boundaries, embracing
everything from jazz to folk. The main components
of this new approach are improvisation, distortion
of sound, extended instrumental solos (especially on
guitar and keyboard), and the incorporation of new
instruments. *Sergeant Pepper*, which comes to be
known as the "psychedelic" album for the Beatles, bears
a photo of Timothy Leary along with many other faces on
its cover. The psychedelic movement also shows its influence
in the graphic arts, especially in posters announcing pop-
music festivals, peace demonstrations, and other
"happenings." Amid all this innovation, the Beatles, who only
recently were on the cutting edge, begin to seem, to some at
least, almost outmoded.

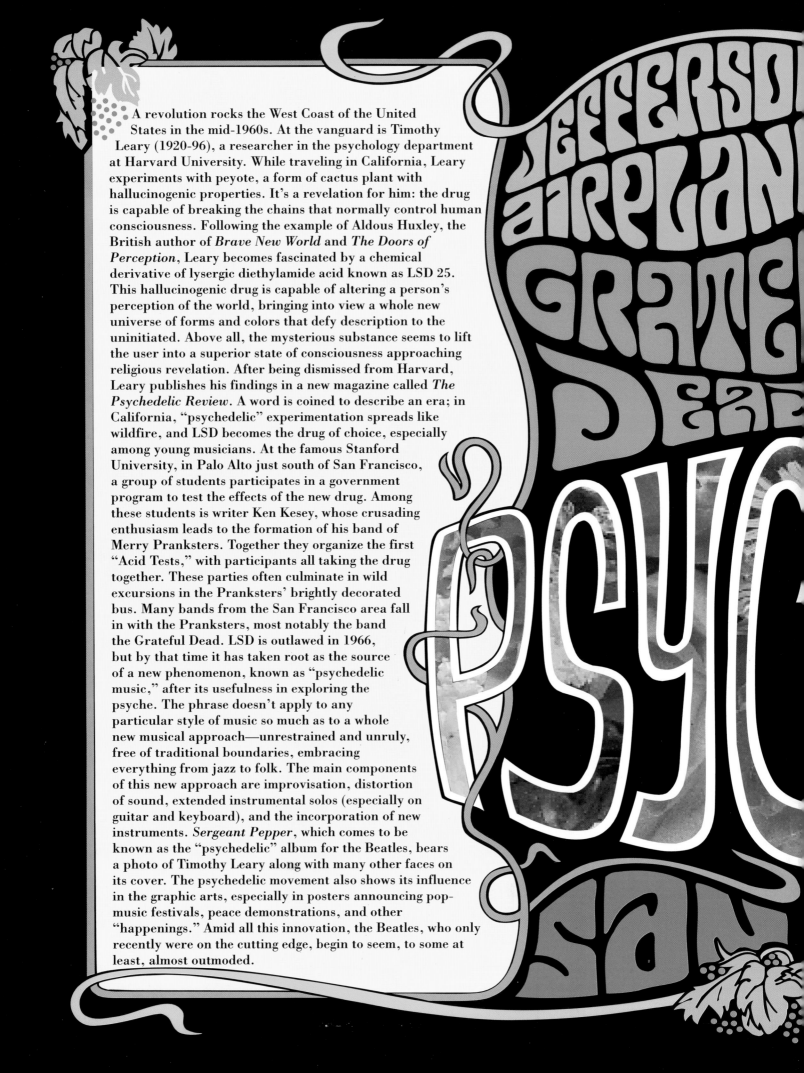

COUNTRY JOE AND THE FISH
QUICKSILVER MESSENGER SERVICE
THE DOORS
BIG BROTHER AND THE HOLDING CO.
JIMI HENDRIX
FRANCISC

People tend to contrast the sweetness of the Beatles with the naughtiness of the Rolling Stones in the mid-1960s. Just a few years later, it is the sweetness of Paul versus the naughtiness of John. Though almost all of the Beatles' songs are credited to "Lennon-McCartney," few result from true collaboration. "A Hard Day's Night," "Help!" "Norwegian Wood," "Strawberry Fields Forever," and "Come Together" come completely from John. "Can't Buy Me Love," "Yesterday," "Drive My Car,"

"Penny Lane," "Lady Madonna," and "Hey Jude" are purely Paul's inventions. The two artists help each other out with advice, offering various touches to perfect each song, but only on rare occasions do they actually write songs together, notable examples being "With a Little Help from My Friends," sung by Ringo, and "A Day in the Life," mainly composed by John but with melody and words by Paul. By around 1967, John and Paul have begun to drift apart. By 1969, the separation is nearly complete, though the band is still

FOR YOURSELF

officially together. John is recording avant-garde albums with Yoko Ono, protesting against the war in Vietnam, and generally rebelling against society. John's hardcore fans belittle Paul's pleasant melodies, which, while appealing to parents, strike John's fans as inane and schmaltzy, peddling conventional and "conformist" platitudes. John is seen as the tortured genius, beset by violent emotions, ill at ease, drawn to the weird and outrageous; it is he who leads the band into troubled waters, with his surrealistic cackling in "I Am the Walrus" and the aggression of "Happiness Is a Warm Gun." Paul can be seen as John's flip side, with his generally sunny disposition and his satisfaction with life's simpler pleasures, even if his songs include the occasional melancholy emotion. In any case, the magical mixture of light and dark helps create some of the most memorable songs of a generation, and though they may not write every song together, Paul and John's influence on each other is immeasurable.

SERGEANT PEPPER; OR, THE BIRTH OF ROCK CULTURE

In the mid-1960s, rock music is still spread mainly through the medium of 45-r.p.m. records, called "singles" when they feature one title (accompanied by a lesser tune on the "B" side), and "EP" (extended-play) records that typically contain four songs. At this time, "LP" (long-playing) record albums are still generally reserved for jazz, classical, or other "adult" musical genres; rock recordings are lumped in the category of "light music" for dancing. The early Beatles albums are released in conformity with this system. Albums like *Beatles '65* contain assorted cover tunes of American rock 'n' roll and R & B standards with original compositions mixed in, all done in a relatively singular style. *A Hard Day's Night* comes straight off the movie soundtrack, in the manner of Elvis Presley's albums. *Help!* is assembled in the same fashion. Innovation arrives with *Rubber Soul*, released in late 1965. For one thing, the songs are generally slower in tempo, making them less adaptable as dance tunes. But also, for the first time in a rock album, there is a real variety of styles, from "Norwegian Wood," with its Indian sitar accompaniment, to "In My Life," with its strikingly dissonant melodic hook and George Martin's classical-sounding harpsichord solo (actually an electric piano recorded at half-speed). *Revolver*, released in the summer of 1966, goes even further, setting the melodic "Eleanor Rigby" alongside the psychedelic effects of "Tomorrow Never Knows." With *Sergeant Pepper's Lonely Hearts Club Band*, which appears in June 1967, the Beatles bring pop music into its full maturity. For the first time, an entire album is conceived as an integral whole, to be heard straight through in the manner of a variety show or even light opera, which in many ways it parodies. The playful album cover promises a "cast of thousands" and features the Beatles dressed in full regimental finery—but with a psychedelic twist. The Beatles have changed from rock musicians into magicians who conjure up potions of sound within the mystical confines of their Abbey Road studios. Each song becomes a world in

miniature, with its
own unique colors
and poetry.
Recorded over a
five-month period within a
(then astounding) budget of
25,000 pounds sterling,
Sergeant Pepper is rock's
first "concept album" and
comes complete with song
lyrics printed in the liner
notes—a major novelty that
will become a standard
feature of the recording
industry by the early 1970s. Lennon's colorful and highly symbolic lyrics invite
interpretation, and songs like "Lucy in the Sky With Diamonds" or "A Day in
the Life" bristle with esoteric and drug-inspired allusions. Playing a rock
album becomes an event that demands undivided attention; listeners sit in their
rooms by candlelight, alone or with close friends, and search for hidden
meanings that might offer the key to poetic or spiritual enlightenment. Before
Sergeant Pepper, rock music was a form of entertainment. Now it is culture.
Not everyone takes rock seriously as a serious art form—at least not yet—but
that's another story.

WITHIN YOU WITHOUT YOU

In the top years of the Beatles' popularity, young people in Britain and America begin burning incense and exploring the mystic religions of the East. In fact, the Beatles are at least partly responsible for this. George Harrison leads the way when he takes off for Bombay at the end of 1966 to take lessons in the sitar (an Indian stringed instrument) from Ravi Shankar. He and his wife, Patti, have suddenly become fascinated with Eastern mysticism, and they embark on a spiritual quest to discover the meaning of life, seeking out new paths toward peace of mind. In August 1967, George leads the other three Beatles to a conference with the Maharishi Mahesh Yogi, an Indian guru who, as head of the International Meditation Society, instructs Westerners in the techniques of transcendental meditation. The Beatles and their friends are charmed by this plump little man with his long hair and wispy beard. With his childish laughter, the Maharishi seems to possess the key to mortal happiness. The band then rushes off to a seminar the Maharishi organizes in Bangor, in the north of Wales, bringing Mick Jagger of the Rolling Stones along with them in their chartered bus. Six months later, with wives and children in tow, they are reunited with Maharishi at his ashram (religious dwelling) in Rishikesh, in the foothills of the Himalayas, for a retreat that lasts several weeks. The program includes yoga, meditation, daily walks, and a vegetarian diet, not to mention oppressive heat and insects of every kind. The Beatles, especially John, have naively come to expect that the Maharishi will somehow hand them some magic formula that would empower them to answer all of life's vexing questions. Naturally, they wait in vain. Holy or not, the Maharishi is letting them down. Meanwhile, his interest in actress Mia Farrow, who was present along with the Beatles at Rishikesh, seems inappropriate at best. The Beatles begin to suspect that the Maharishi is less interested in the band members themselves than in the profit and publicity he garners through his relationship with them. "We made a mistake," Paul concludes. "We thought there was more to him than there was. He's human. We thought at first that he wasn't."

GETTING BETTER ALL THE TIME

The new so-called consumer society (an expression that dates to the 1960s) is driven by advertising and publicity. One of the great discoveries of marketers is the value of giving the consumer the illusion of choice. For example, supermarket shelves offer shoppers a vast assortment of different brands of detergent, and thanks to ads consumers become loyal users of one product (unaware that most contain exactly the same powder or liquid, sometimes even manufactured at the same plant). Modern packaging, with its bright colors and exuberant vitality, transforms shopping into an exciting adventure.

And with the increasing prosperity of the 1960s a host of exciting new labor-saving devices arrive, each designed to ease the burdens of housekeeping and free up more time for recreation. Ever-changing fashions affect not just clothing but all aspects of daily life, and keeping up with the latest styles means constantly replacing "old stuff" as new products come on the market. This trend accelerates during the 1960s, and by the end of the decade critics are lamenting the new phenomenon of "planned obsolescence" as well as the increasing impact on the environment of wasteful consumption.

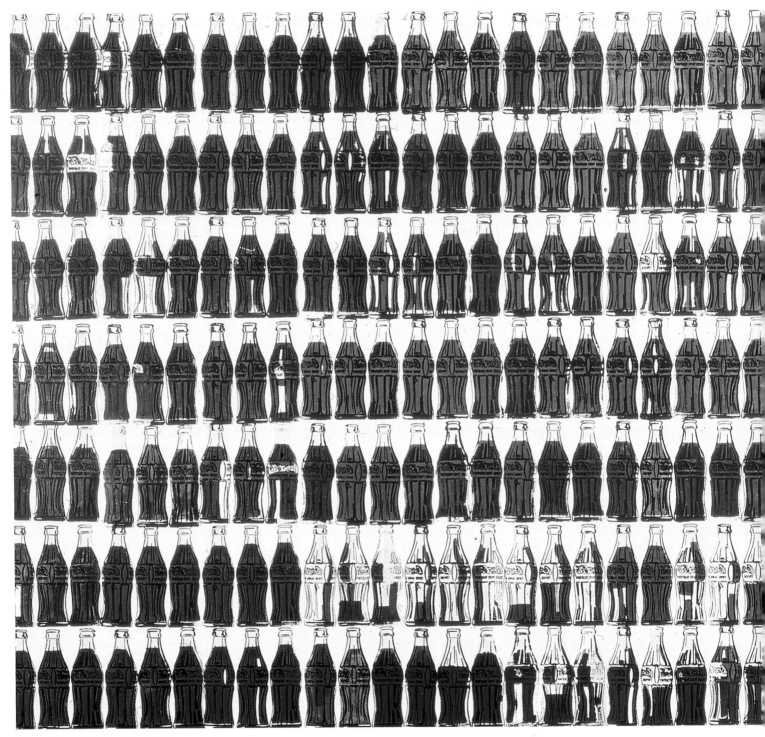

Green Coca-Cola bottles, *1962*,
by Andy Warhol.

- **ANDY WARHOL**
- **ROY LICHTENSTEIN**
- **TOM WESSELMANN**
- **JAMES ROSENQUIST**
- **JASPER JOHNS**
- **CLAES OLDENBURG**

- **JIM DINE**
- **ROBERT RAUSCHENBERG**
- **ALLEN JONES**
- **PETER BLAKE**
- **EDUARDO PAOLOZZI**
- **RICHARD HAMILTON**

EVERYWHERE

"Everything is beautiful" because "life is art." Such formulas express the philosophy of the American painter Andy Warhol, whose new aesthetic vision comes to be known as pop art. In twentieth-century art, which grows out of modern European philosophical conceptions, art comes to be seen as an affirmation of individual subjectivity; the artist imposes his personal vision on

Lichtenstein, whose oversized reproductions of comic-book characters in melodramatic situations are executed with painterly precision. The underlying message is one of despair in the face of a society all too tolerant, even worshipful, of hollow, impersonal images. The Beatles, for their part, interpret pop art with a sense of optimism. It is possible, after all, to see

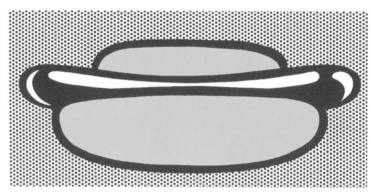

Roy Lichtenstein

the rest of society. Warhol's idealized images of soup cans, Coca-Cola bottles, comic strips, and Marilyn Monroe are plucked out of the mass media and reproduced as art objects in themselves. By presenting these images in a way that forces the viewer to see them out of context, Warhol instantly transforms the tools of mass merchandising into cultural icons. Pop art sells nothing but images, images that previously had no value beyond their ability to sell merchandise. With a strong sense of irony and paradox, Warhol holds a mirror up to modern society by accentuating the absurd scenery of an increasingly commercial culture. Warhol's canvases exude irony and skepticism, as do those of Roy

humor, poetry, and beauty in the stuff of popular culture. There is no need to reject anything. In 1967, the Beatles ask Peter Blake, a 35-year-old English artist who creates collages of illustrations from popular magazines, to do the cover for *Sergeant Pepper*. The next year, they choose Richard Hamilton to design to cover for *The Beatles*. Hamilton's answer to the overstated colors of the psychedelic style is to wrap the exterior of this new double album in total blankness and grace the interior gatefold with an insert of four full-color, close-up portraits of the individual Beatles, along with a large collage. In the years that follow, Warhol himself contributes an album cover design for the Rolling Stones.

- NIKI DE SAINT PHALLE
- ARMAN
- MARTIAL RAYSSE
- CHRISTO

POP ART

WHO'S GOING TO CARRY THAT WEIGHT?

The news comes at the end of August 1967, while the four Beatles are attending the Maharishi's seminar in Bangor, Wales: Brian Epstein, their manager, has been discovered lying lifeless in his bed. An autopsy gives the cause of death as an overdose of sleeping pills and barbiturates. The Beatles feel orphaned. "We'd never have made it without him, and vice-versa," John later says. "We were the talent, but *he* was the hustler." The band's decision in 1966 to stop playing concert tours left Epstein feeling useless to them. By nature the tormented, loner type, Epstein had come to depend on the Beatles as family, and he dreaded the day when they might no longer need him. But ironically, things will never be the same again for the Beatles after Epstein's death. Turning to less competent advisors, the Beatles launch into a succession of risky business ventures, one being the creation of the Apple company, which unfortunately proves to be a financial drain. In 1969, in a desperate attempt to shore up their sagging finances, the Beatles hire Allen Klein, an American businessman, but the result is heightened tension among the four musicians. Whether by chance or consequence, the death of Brian Epstein, coming as it does at the height of their success with *Sergeant Pepper,* marks the beginning of a slow but steady decline in the band's ability to function as a cohesive unit. The old feeling of togetherness is gone, never to return. When the time comes to lay down tracks for their next double album, *The Beatles* (better known as "The White Album"), the band members begin working separately, taking turns in the recording studio. But Epstein's death, as often happens with the death of a father figure, can also be seen as having its liberating effects on the individual Beatles, releasing them from the prison of the team and encouraging each to assert his individuality. George goes on to make his own recording of Indian music in 1968 for a film entitled *Wonderwall*; John soon begins work on an album of experimental music with Yoko Ono. The die is cast. After so many years of seamless musical teamwork, the most successful band in history is beginning to come apart.

TELL ME

Until the mid-1960s, rock 'n' roll music exists only on the radio and records: there are no music videos and nothing at all like MTV. The Beatles can be seen live, on television—or in movie theaters, and their movies change everything. Their first movie, *A Hard Day's Night*, is released in the summer of 1964. The film is directed by the young American filmmaker Richard Lester. The script is by Alun Owen, a Liverpool screenwriter inspired by the laconic humor and deadpan antics of the Beatles who always seem to keep a cool head, even amid the chaos of their delirious fans. The whimsical story line reminds film critics of Marx Brothers movies. Their next movie, *Help!* is also directed by Lester and comes out the following year. It has a larger budget, which lets Mr. Lester spice things up with the gadgetry typical of a James Bond movie, wild plot twists, and burlesque comedy.

Early in 1967 the BBC asks the Beatles to supply a short film to promote "Strawberry Fields Forever," which is released as a 45-r.p.m. (with "Penny Lane" on the "B" side). They turn to a Swedish director named Peter

WHAT YOU SEE

Goldmann, who had worked with the English folk singer Donovan, to make the film. Goldmann decides to shoot at night in a park, suspending an organ from trees by huge ropes to create a surrealistic scene. The Beatles run back and forth in sped-up fast motion.

When they direct their own TV movie, *Magical Mystery Tour*, at the end of the same year, the Beatles stick with their bizarre antics: a city bus painted in a rainbow of bright colors, manned by a cheerful crew and followed by dwarf wrestlers, motorcyclists, five clergymen, and a rugby team. John has a dream: dressed up as a waiter with slicked-back hair, he uses a shovel to serve spaghetti to an obese woman. The four Beatles appear later in magician's garb with animal masks and play "I Am the Walrus" in front of a giant wall surmounted by a line of dancing police officers. Here again, the Beatles are way ahead of their time, as if looking into their crystal ball and prophesying the future trend of music videos.

1967: WORKING IT OUT

1967, year of *Sergeant Pepper,* is the highwater mark for the success of the Beatles. America and Europe are at the peak of prosperity. How are people really doing?

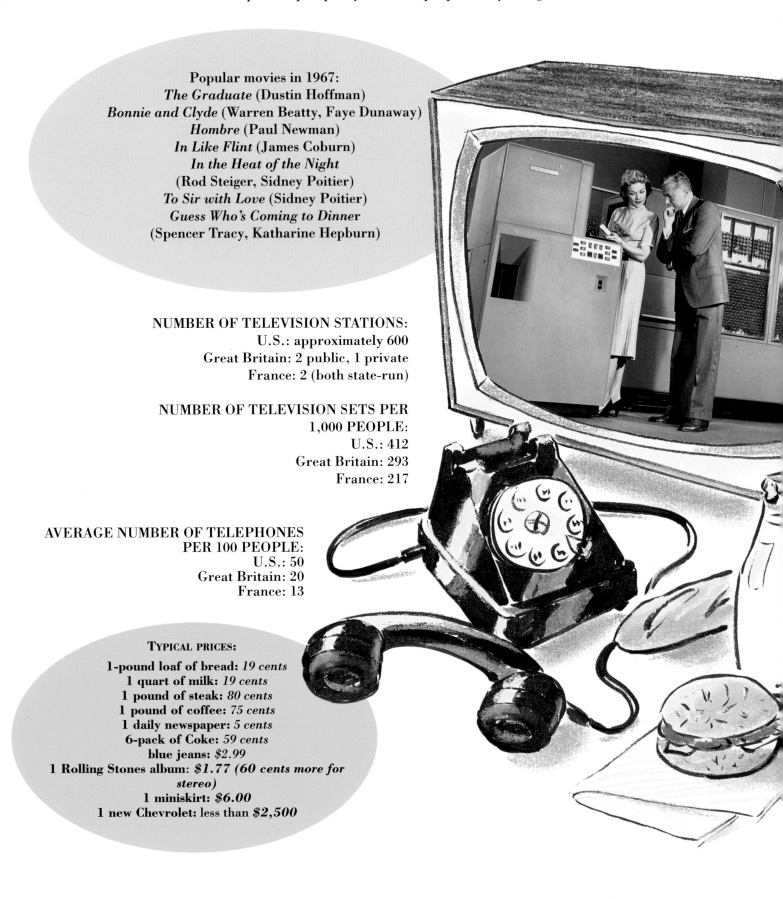

Popular movies in 1967:
The Graduate (Dustin Hoffman)
Bonnie and Clyde (Warren Beatty, Faye Dunaway)
Hombre (Paul Newman)
In Like Flint (James Coburn)
In the Heat of the Night
(Rod Steiger, Sidney Poitier)
To Sir with Love (Sidney Poitier)
Guess Who's Coming to Dinner
(Spencer Tracy, Katharine Hepburn)

NUMBER OF TELEVISION STATIONS:
U.S.: approximately 600
Great Britain: 2 public, 1 private
France: 2 (both state-run)

NUMBER OF TELEVISION SETS PER
1,000 PEOPLE:
U.S.: 412
Great Britain: 293
France: 217

AVERAGE NUMBER OF TELEPHONES
PER 100 PEOPLE:
U.S.: 50
Great Britain: 20
France: 13

TYPICAL PRICES:
1-pound loaf of bread: *19 cents*
1 quart of milk: *19 cents*
1 pound of steak: *80 cents*
1 pound of coffee: *75 cents*
1 daily newspaper: *5 cents*
6-pack of Coke: *59 cents*
blue jeans: *$2.99*
1 Rolling Stones album: *$1.77 (60 cents more for
stereo)*
1 miniskirt: *$6.00*
1 new Chevrolet: less than *$2,500*

POPULATION:
U.S.: 200 million
Great Britain: 55 million
France: 49 million

UNEMPLOYMENT RATE:
U.S.: 4.8%
Great Britain: 3%
France: 2.7%

AVERAGE LIFE EXPECTANCY:
Men: 68 years
Women: 75 years

NUMBER OF STUDENTS:
U.S.: 1 million
Great Britain: 300,000
France: 600,000

NUMBER OF RADIOS PER 1,000 PEOPLE:
U.S.: 1,412
Great Britain: 327
France: 318

DON'T EXIST YET:
Video cassette recorders (VCRs), dishwashers,
"Walkman" portable tape players,
fax machines, electronic
calculators, personal computers,
cordless telephones.
EXIST BUT ARE RARE:
Color television sets

In 1967, the British government demands 2 million pounds sterling in taxes from the Beatles. To avoid paying up, their advisors suggest investing the money in a chain of stores. The Beatles approve the idea, but on condition that the stores be uniquely designed as "a beautiful place where you could buy beautiful things." Thus begins, in December 1967, the utopian dream known as Apple—a dream that will soon become a nightmare. In fairness to the Beatles, the climate of the times encourages such wacky fantasies. First they open a boutique in London manned by three hippies who come in from Amsterdam and set up shop to sell a variety of odd gadgets and clothing. The storefront features a psychedelic fresco in rainbow colors. Within a few months, the Beatles have squandered every penny of their investment; they soon decide to close the store, but only after giving away the inventory for free. This sets the tone for all of Apple's enterprises. The Beatles are millionaires who fancy themselves utopian visionaries, and they want to create a company that will offer money and services to aspiring filmmakers, composers of new music, even inventors. Thanks to Apple, announce the Beatles, creators and inventors will no longer have to bow down to "men in suits" who do nothing but sit around in their offices and have no regard for anything except profit-and-loss estimates.

"We've already bought all our dreams, so now we want to share that possibility with others," proclaims Paul. The effect is to attract a tidal wave of eccentrics who line up to present their absurd ideas for new projects. One of these, a young Greek man with a passion for electronics, catches John's attention. He is promptly named to head up a newly created division, called Apple Electronics, and

THIS APPLE BIT BACK

is given all the time and resources he needs to come up with all manner of bizarre gadgets, such as an electric apple that changes colors with the tune of the music. This same crank genius gets it into his head to build, in the basement of the Apple building, a gigantic studio that will supposedly revolutionize the techniques of audio recording. This venture turns out to be a fiasco of prodigious proportions: not one of the planned 78 tracks ever works, and half a million dollars are devoured in the project. The Beatles, swept away by the implausible ideal of "Western communism," dream of creating an independent parcel delivery service, even an alternative school. Their dreams seem to know no bounds.

The awakening is indeed rude. In mid-1969, the American businessman Allen Klein bursts the bubble by laying off all the Apple employees. The company survives until the mid-1970s, but as an ordinary record company. The utopian house of cards has collapsed. Apple is rotten to the core and threatens to spoil the rest of what the Beatles have worked so hard to create.

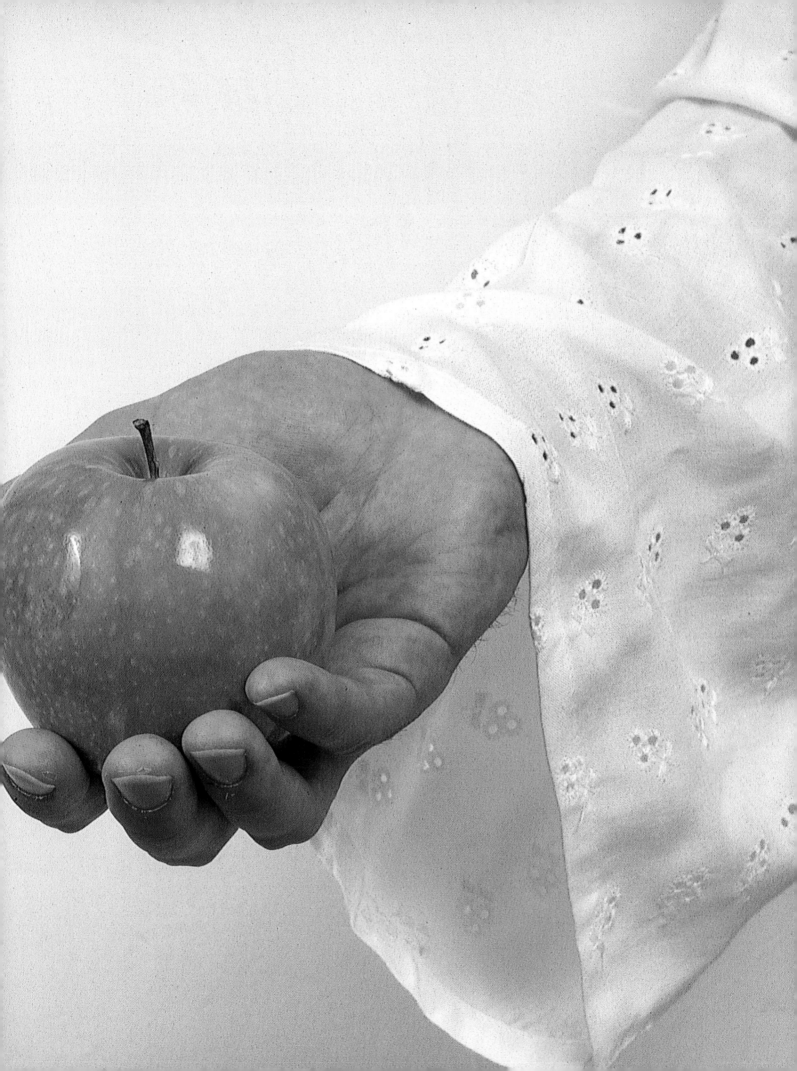

MINI, MINI, MINI

They were causing fender-benders in the streets of
Paris. What were these hazards? Miniskirts! In
1965, a Parisian fashion designer named
Courrèges leaps to fame with a revolutionary
collection: his models wear dresses made from a
single length of fabric, without pleats, cut four or
five inches above the knee. The patterns are
influenced by op art (optical art), which plays on
the dazzling visual effects of high-contrast stripes.
Coco Chanel, leading lady of Parisian fashion,
ridicules this brazen new design. The next year,
Mary Quant, a young stylist from London, goes even
farther when she comes up with the true miniskirt,
shorter than the Courrèges design. It's a shot heard
'round the world. The young women who first don
Quant's miniskirt cause havoc in their homes when
their parents see what they're wearing (or not
wearing). Dad may be amused, if also a bit uneasy, but
Mom is up in arms: "No daughter of mine is setting
foot outside this house looking like that!" Girls who
dare to wear the skirt to school are promptly called
into the principal's office. Those highly adventurous
adults who do their best to keep up with the times try
on these fashions themselves, but make young people
fall down in fits of laughter. It is clear from the outset
that only young girls can really wear miniskirts. The
miniskirt is just another symbol of the younger
generation's increasing hold on popular culture.

It's the mid-1960s: you still can't find a color television in most American homes. High school girls wear uniforms of pleated plaid skirts with matching socks and cardigan sweaters. A checked shirt is about the best any boy can hope for; the rest of his outfit is typically drab gray. But in Paris, fashion designer Courrèges has already planted the seeds of a fashion revolution with his scandalous miniskirt. In "swinging London," designer Mary Quant draws inspiration from the cheerfully unabashed lifestyle of the hip crowd, and her design for an ultra-short miniskirt quickly catches on among trendy women, who wear it with fiery-colored tights, hair cut in bangs, and white makeup with black eyeliner. Thin is "in," and all girls aspire to

GROOVY THREADS

the slinky, androgynous figure of model Twiggy. For the first time, youth has a style it can truly call its own. Carnaby Street, a small side street in London's Soho district, becomes center stage for all the newest fashion trends. Young dandies strut their stuff, sporting the most eccentric clothes and hairstyles. Amid the clothing boutiques and record shops, bustling Carnaby Street has it all—top hats, ruffled shirts, Brandenburg frock jackets, "Mao" outfits, surplus goods from Afghanistan, Nepal, or Peru—and everyone vies to make the most audacious and colorful fashion statement. London's young hipsters are sticking their tongues out at the "Establishment" and its drab uniformity: "Look at you, you're pathetic," they sneer.

Before the 1960s, young people were trained to imitate older people.
From now on, the tables are turned, and adults do
their best to keep up with the kids.

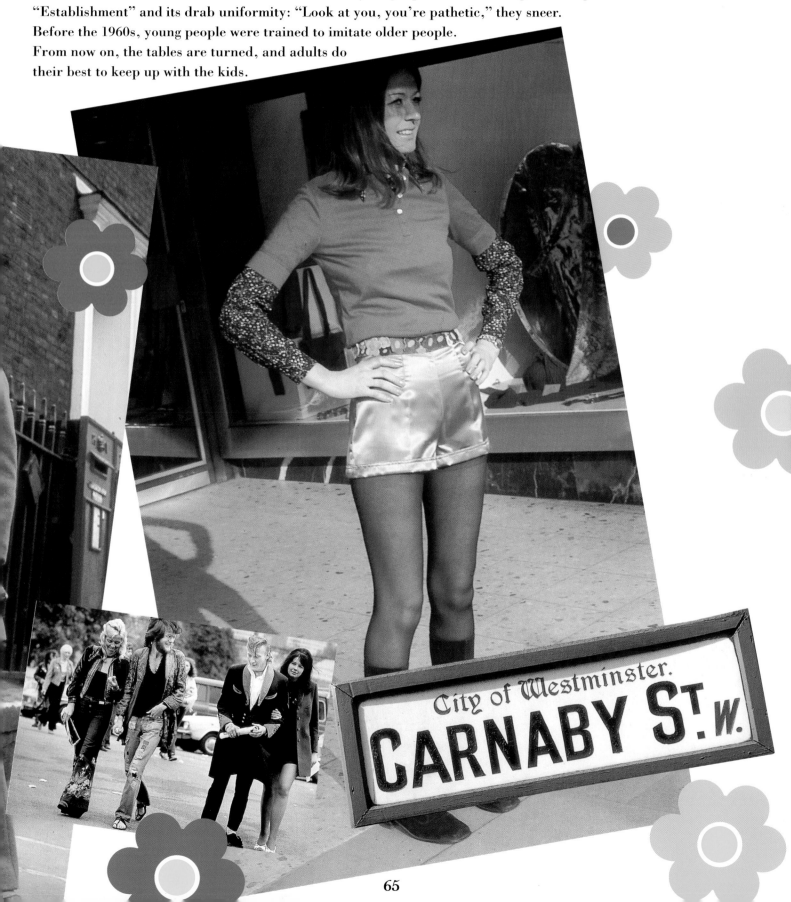

It all happened so fast. Last night at dinner my brother started the usual argument with my father about the war in Vietnam. My brother insisted that American troops are all fascists because they burn innocent Vietnamese alive with napalm. My father responded by accusing my brother of being full of fancy ideas but not knowing what he was talking about. He said my brother should read up on his history. Then my father announced that my brother was grounded. Just like that. At that point my brother turned red in the face and started screaming at my father, saying it was no surprise that he supported fascists, since he was one himself. He said he could care less about exams and school, that all his teachers were "idiots" (that's exactly what he said), that he wanted to take off on a trip faraway from "all this junk" (he said something worse). "Oh, sure," said my father, who was trying to stay calm despite his anger, even though he seemed to have forgotten to chew the food in his mouth. "And what are you going to use for money?" "Money, money, money," cried my brother. "I don't care about money! I'll hitch rides, or I'll hop trains, and I'll go live with my friends, and we'll share everything. We don't need a telephone or a car or any of that!" Then he started complaining about how our neighbor, Jerry, is allowed to go out every night and how his father gave him a car. "And I can't even go out on Sunday! That's completely mindless!" Then he threw down his napkin and stormed off to his room. My father and mother looked at each other and sighed. I asked them if I could finish the piece of pie left on my brother's plate. They said that would be just fine.

IT'S ONLY LOVE

In his youth, John nourished a dream of becoming a painter. As an adult, he continues to make drawings in his spare time. In addition, his pursuits as a poet result in the publication of two books of verse, *In His Own Write* in 1964 and *A Spaniard in the Works* the next year. When he meets Yoko Ono, a Japanese performance artist based in London, he finds a guide to the avant-garde of artistic experimentation. For one of her "performances," Ono sits in a gallery and enlists the help of visitors in cutting off her clothing with a pair of scissors. Yoko comes from a wealthy banking family and is 33 years old when she meets John (he's 26). When they're introduced in November 1966, she is hardly aware of who he is. Their artistic collaboration soon yields *Two Virgins*, a musical collage of noises that is released at the end of 1968; this "event" is notable less for the music itself than for the album cover, which shows the couple stark naked facing the camera. All of the projects they undertake together—films, experimental music, a week-long "love-in" for peace spent entirely in bed—are marked by a similar exhibitionism before the media. This is no less true of their marriage, which takes the form of a public "happening." In the summer of 1968, during the recording of *The Beatles* (the "White Album"), John and Yoko make a mutual decision to spend every minute together from then on. When Yoko falls ill, a bed is set up for her in the studio so she can be there to help John during his recording sessions. In early 1969, when the four Beatles decide to reunite in the studio to film the documentary *Let It Be*, storm clouds are already gathering on the horizon, and the uninterrupted presence of Yoko in the studio doesn't help matters. The British press, with its typically misogynist attitude, accuses this "witch" of sowing discord among the band members. Many fans agree. For his part, John voices his opinion that after Brian Epstein's death, the entire band knew right away that their days were numbered—an accusation that never quite goes away. Between John and Yoko, there will be complete oneness to the end. At one point John decides to rebaptize himself John Ono Lennon, and some psychoanalyze this as a way for him, who barely knew his mother, to retie an umbilical cord that was cut far too early.

After the death of their manager, Brian Epstein, in August 1967, the Beatles feel abandoned and completely disoriented. In an attempt to find themselves again, they set off to India for a sojourn at the ashram of the Maharishi Mahesh Yogi in the foothills of the Himalayas. The experience has the opposite effect of what they intended, and they are left feeling further isolated from one another. While the others return to England, George stays and takes sitar lessons from Ravi Shankar in preparation for an album of Indian music entitled *Wonderwall*. Back in London, John launches into experimental music and cinema with Yoko Ono. Ringo tries his hand at movie acting and even flirts with the idea of quitting the band altogether. Paul is left to hold down the fort and begins to feel like the only real Beatle left.

The process of recording the double-album *The Beatles* (also known as the "White Album") in 1968 reveals deep unrest within the band, especially when the band members begin going into the studio one at a time for separate recording sessions. Despite the triumphant success of "Hey Jude" and the "White Album" as a whole, the Beatles seem weakened and prey to doubt. Paul finally sounds the alarm when he voices his wish to record a new album immediately and to do it the way they used to early on, in the true rock 'n' roll spirit of speed and spontaneity. He even suggests going back on stage for several public concerts. Meanwhile, the band is under a contractual obligation to put out another film, and Paul puts forth the idea of killing two birds with one stone by hiring a crew to film the band as they record their next album, a project provisionally entitled *Get Back*.

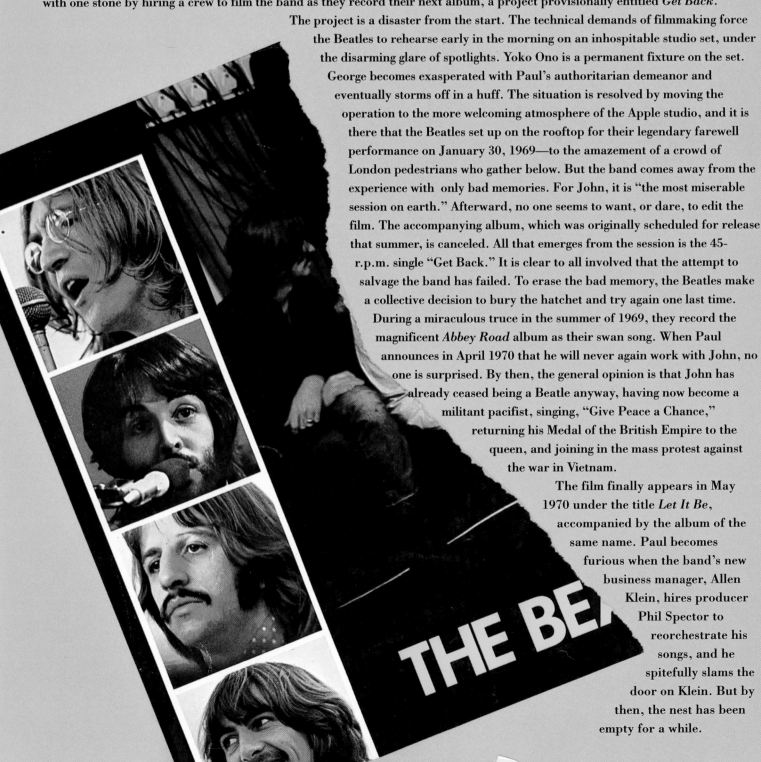

The project is a disaster from the start. The technical demands of filmmaking force the Beatles to rehearse early in the morning on an inhospitable studio set, under the disarming glare of spotlights. Yoko Ono is a permanent fixture on the set. George becomes exasperated with Paul's authoritarian demeanor and eventually storms off in a huff. The situation is resolved by moving the operation to the more welcoming atmosphere of the Apple studio, and it is there that the Beatles set up on the rooftop for their legendary farewell performance on January 30, 1969—to the amazement of a crowd of London pedestrians who gather below. But the band comes away from the experience with only bad memories. For John, it is "the most miserable session on earth." Afterward, no one seems to want, or dare, to edit the film. The accompanying album, which was originally scheduled for release that summer, is canceled. All that emerges from the session is the 45-r.p.m. single "Get Back." It is clear to all involved that the attempt to salvage the band has failed. To erase the bad memory, the Beatles make a collective decision to bury the hatchet and try again one last time. During a miraculous truce in the summer of 1969, they record the magnificent *Abbey Road* album as their swan song. When Paul announces in April 1970 that he will never again work with John, no one is surprised. By then, the general opinion is that John has already ceased being a Beatle anyway, having now become a militant pacifist, singing, "Give Peace a Chance," returning his Medal of the British Empire to the queen, and joining in the mass protest against the war in Vietnam.

The film finally appears in May 1970 under the title *Let It Be*, accompanied by the album of the same name. Paul becomes furious when the band's new business manager, Allen Klein, hires producer Phil Spector to reorchestrate his songs, and he spitefully slams the door on Klein. But by then, the nest has been empty for a while.

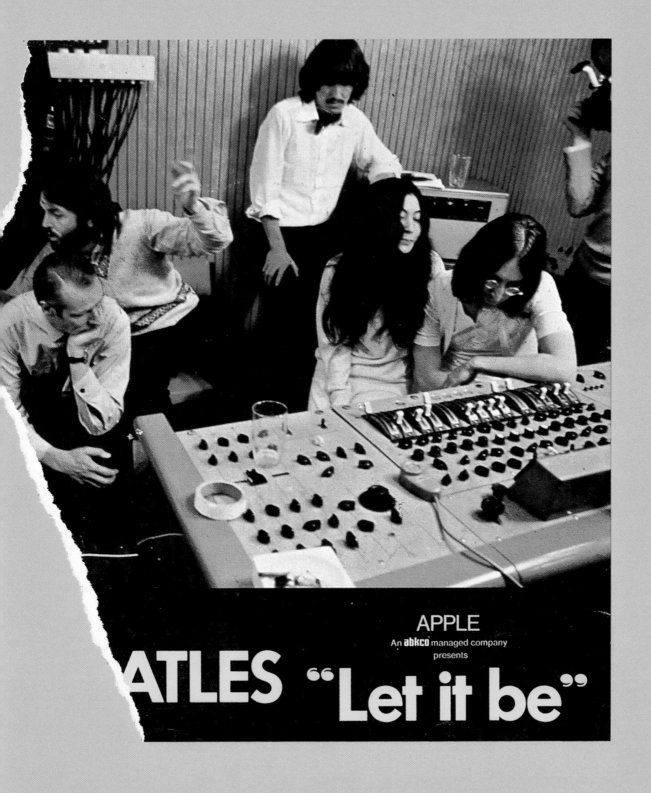

PATHFINDERS OF DREAMS

"We were all on this ship in the sixties, our generation, a ship going to discover the New World. And the Beatles were in the crow's nest of that ship. . . . We were part of it and contributed what we contributed; I can't designate what we did and didn't do. It depends on how each individual was impressed by the Beatles or how our shock wave went to different people. We were going through the changes, and all we were saying was, it's raining up here, or there's land or there's sun or we can see a seagull. We were just reporting what was happening to us."
—John, 1974

All You Need Is Love

Love, love, love, love, love, love, love, love, love.
There's nothing that you can do that can't be done.
Nothing you can sing that can't be sung.

A.D. 2000: WILL YOU STILL FEED ME? WILL YOU STILL NEED ME?

It's taken for granted in the 1960s that life will be better and different by the end of the millennium. Work, leisure, housing, transportation, even clothing are sure to be transformed nearly beyond recognition. Robots will replace human laborers in factories. People will live in bubbles, underground or underwater, protected from the weather. Commuters will travel in ultra-high-speed trains humming along on cushions of air. As for clothes, there will be metallic suits with glass-visored helmets like those of astronauts. Thanks to the miraculous pace of medical progress, the human lifespan will approach virtual immortality; even brain transplants will be within the realm of possibility. The progress of technology seems so rapid that even the most outlandish inventions are discussed as if they are just around the corner. After all, back in the 1930s, who would have believed men would be walking on the moon? Why shouldn't it be possible to colonize the entire solar system by the year 2000? Or build entire cities in outer space? Who could deny that every family might someday possess its own spaceship, allowing Mom and Pop to take the kids for a picnic on Mars? In 1968, filmmaker Stanley Kubrick's *2001: A Space Odyssey* offers a vision of the future that is both fascinating and menacing. The movie features a futuristic space vessel that gradually falls under the control of its on-board computer, to the point where the crew has little power at all over the functions of the ship. Of course, all this is pure fantasy in the 1960s. For the average person everyday life has changed very little in terms of its essentials. Large suburban housing projects are beginning to appear, but for the most

part, the look of the towns and countryside is much as it has always
been. There has been a revolution in transportation, of course, and
clothing, food, and furnishings have been gradually transformed as
creature comforts are distributed more and more democratically, and
the daily life of the average citizen has become less arduous. But on the
whole, people's basic values and preferences haven't changed much.
Most of the countries of Europe are still predominantly rural. In
retrospect, the changes of the 1960s seem to have been as much
imagined as real. And when, in the decade of the 1970s, many of these
changes do in fact take place, the dream of the future loses much of its
sparkle. Before long, people begin looking back with nostalgia at the
lost Golden Age—a simpler and more innocent past when wasteful
consumption hadn't yet marred the planet and despoiled its resources
and people were still content with what nature offered on its own.

1954-58: THE BIRTH OF ROCK 'N' ROLL
Rock 'n' roll is born in the U.S.A. The term itself, popularized by Cleveland disc jockey Alan Freed, describes a revolution: for the first time, young white people are playing and singing a form of the rhythm-and-blues music of American blacks. Rock 'n' roll is thus a hybrid, a blend of black blues, rhythm and blues, and gospel music, and white country and western music. In 1956, Elvis Presley becomes the king of this new rock 'n' roll revolution, with Gene Vincent, Jerry Lee Lewis, Eddie Cochran, and Buddy Holly also leading the charge. Black singers like Chuck Berry, Little Richard, Ray Charles, and Fats Domino have an equally great influence on their successors, including the Beatles.

1958-62: ROCK 'N' ROLL INVADES EUROPE
By March 1958, when Elvis is drafted into the U.S. Army, rock 'n' roll has become a solid fad, with strong commercial potential, and record companies are beginning to manufacture teen idols from a cookie-cutter mold, yielding such aseptic stars as Fabian and Frankie Avalon. In England, the likes of Cliff Richard, Billy Fury, and Tommy Steele compete to take over leadership of the rock 'n' roll revolution. In France, crowds are demanding to hear Johnny Hallyday, at times even to the point of riots that attract not just the police but the attention of General Charles De Gaulle himself.

1965: THE BIRTH OF FOLK ROCK
The American music industry reacts quickly to the British Invasion. The transformation is made clear when Bob Dylan, known for his poetic folk songs and social protest songs, appears at the Newport Folk Festival backed by a rock band. The Byrds come out with Beatles-inspired electric versions of protest songs. Rock bands spring up overnight, soon embarking on world tours. The Lovin' Spoonful, Mamas and the Papas, Turtles, and others mix the raw energy of rock with the melodic strains of American folk music: folk rock is the new wave.

1966: THE EXPLOSION OF BLACK MUSIC
For the first time, great black stars like James Brown and Otis Redding begin delivering their straight-ahead rhythm sounds to young white audiences with no pretense of softening their style for white America. This inspiring music comes to be called soul music.

1961-64: BIRTH OF THE PROTEST SONG

In New York, another revolution is gathering its forces. Pete Seeger, Joan Baez, and Bob Dylan are singing in coffee houses, expressing antiestablishment sentiments in their poetic lyrics and using only their acoustic guitars to back them up. They wield each song like a political weapon against racism, the arms race, and the escalating war in Vietnam. Protest songs, as they come to be called, are songs of commitment and courage. Around the world, young protesters take up guitars to sing out their rebellion against the old establishment.

1964: THE BRITISH INVASION

After deteriorating into fodder for teeny-boppers, rock 'n' roll has been left for dead in the U.S.A. But its roots in the blues and R & B continue to find nourishment across the ocean in the urban caves of London, in the hands of the Rolling Stones, the Animals, Manfred Mann, and other young rockers. Americans are later astonished to rediscover their own musical origins through the contributions of several talented young British artists who recapture the rage and savage passion of early R & B artists. Soon the Yardbirds, the Kinks, the Small Faces, the Who, and then Cream, with Eric Clapton, all make their mark on the evolution of this distinctly American genre.

1967-68: BIRTH OF PSYCHEDELIC ROCK

In San Francisco, a movement is afoot to bring together music and mind-altering drugs like LSD. On the West Coast, bands like the Grateful Dead, Jefferson Airplane, Quicksilver Messenger Service, and the Doors lace their music with extended improvisations and calls for inner emancipation. The hippies have arrived. In turn, British bands like Pink Floyd and Soft Machine take their inspiration from these American innovators.

1968-70: THE BLUES BOOM AND THE POP MUSIC REVOLUTION

Woodstock, the legendary rock festival held in August 1969, proves that rock has achieved the status of a new religion capable of rallying masses of the faithful. The late 1960s is a heady time for pop music, and is also a preview of what is to come in the next decade: the revival of electric blues with Canned Heat and Fleetwood Mac; blues-rock; the hard rock of Led Zeppelin; King Crimson and the birth of "progressive" rock, with its assimilation of the classical symphonic tradition; jazz improvisation and avant-garde electronic music; and a variety of new Latin rhythms, notably in the music of Carlos Santana. Jimi Hendrix uses his outstanding musical genius to create a unique fusion of the blues, rock, psychedelic music, and jazz. When the smoke of the 1960s clears, rock music continues on its planetary orbit.

REVOL

At
the great rock festivals—Woodstock in
Upstate New York or those on England's Isle of Wight—
couples kiss passionately in the open without embarrassment. Some even
make love in the middle of the crowd. For hippies and others, unrepressed
sexuality means deliverance from society's taboos. Magazines and leaflets guide young
people in discovery of their own bodies, the goal being mastery of sexual enjoyment. Anything
that heightens sexual pleasure is encouraged. For most people, of course, the notion of sexual
liberation in the 1960s is far removed from daily reality. At the average high school, for example, a
couple daring enough to hold hands or kiss in the hall would cause a scandal and probably risk getting
expelled. And at home, parents, of course, rule. In the 1960s, the expectations of most young women
were limited: get married, have children, stay home to take care of the family. Domestic tasks were
still considered a woman's primary occupation. But changes were coming; some women began to
revolt. The birth control pill allowed women far more control over contraception than ever
before. Taking their destiny into their own hands, women began clamoring for equal
rights, especially the right to equal pay for equal work. Throughout the 1960s,
for many reasons, authority figures were losing much of their power,
but women came out of the decade with increased power,
a result of the rise of feminist values.

UTION !

"IT GOES LIKE THIS . . ."

A HARD DAY'S NIGHT

It's been a hard day's night,
And I've been working like a dog

This song, its title used for the Beatles' first film, was released in June 1964 and is one of the band's best known. The title came from one of Ringo's typical malapropisms. One evening, exhausted after the day's filming, he said, "It's been a hard day" and then, looking out the window and noticing that darkness had fallen, changed "day" into "day's night."

HELP!

Help! I need somebody, help!
Not just anybody, help!
You know I need someone, help!

The title song of the Beatles' second film, this was released in July 1965. John's lyrics were sincere: despite the sudden success of the Beatles, and all the fame and money that came along with it—or perhaps because of all that—John felt unhappy and dispirited. Beneath the song's joyful beat lurks a real cry for help.

LUCY IN THE SKY
WITH DIAMONDS

Picture yourself in a boat on a river,
With tangerine trees and marmalade skies

Many people have long claimed that John wrote this song about LSD, which are the initials of the song's title. This legend will probably never die, but the true inspiration for the title came from a drawing by John's young son Julian showing Lucy, Julian's schoolteacher, "in the sky with diamonds."

NOWHERE MAN

He's a real nowhere man,
Sitting in his nowhere land,
Making all his nowhere plans for nobody

This song, written by John for the album *Rubber Soul*, seems to refer to John himself. The first Beatles song not about love, "Nowhere Man" describes a moment of despair and emptiness.

IN MY LIFE

There are places I'll remember,
All my life though some have changed,
Some forever, not for better,
Some have gone and some remain

This poignantly nostalgic song is among the most personal ever written by John. Its opening promise of a list of some the people and places of his Liverpool past yields to a more abstract evocation of their memories.

ELEANOR RIGBY

Eleanor Rigby picks up the rice in a
church where a wedding has been

This song's haunting melody was written by Paul and set to the accompaniment of a string section with the help of George Martin. The name in the title is imaginary; Paul claimed to have made it up, but there was a Rigby family in Liverpool, and an Eleanor Rigby (1895-1939) is buried in a Liverpool churchyard. Perhaps it came to Paul as a memory unconsciously recalled from a walk taken in years past.

YELLOW SUBMARINE

In the town where I was born,
Lived a man who sailed the sea

Countless children have learned this song by heart, and it ranks among the most familiar Beatles tunes. Paul wrote it as a children's song, and although some people have seen allusions to LSD in the lyrics of this colorful ditty, he has always strenuously denied any such references.

SERGEANT PEPPER'S LONELY
HEARTS CLUB BAND

It was twenty years ago today,
That Sergeant Pepper taught the band to
play

These are the opening lines of the most famous Beatles album. The imaginary band was invented by Paul, cleverly parodying some of the rock groups then playing on America's West Coast, like Big Brother and the Holding Company or Quicksilver Messenger Service. *Sergeant Pepper's* psychedelic elements appealed to the taste of the day, and its opening fanfare of trumpets and canned applause lend a comical air to the album.

YESTERDAY

Yesterday, all my troubles seemed
so far away,
Now it looks as though they're here to stay

One morning in 1965, while in London, Paul woke up with a fully formed melody in his head. He sat down at the piano and played "Yesterday," the tune that had come to him in his sleep as if by some magical spell.

BEATLES LYRICS

A Day in the Life

I read the news today, oh boy,
About a lucky man who made the grade

This song includes John's celebrated phrase, "I'd love to turn you on," which got the song banned from the radio airwaves for what the BBC alleged was a drug reference.

I Am the Walrus

I am he,
As you are he,
As you are me,

And
we are all
together

This bizarre masterpiece with its famous "GOO GOO GOO JOOB" lyrics (supposedly a walrus's cry) was apparently John Lennon's attempt to foil those fans who were bent on analyzing every line of every Beatles song—an increasingly popular pursuit at the time. In fact, the lyrics appear to be a string of absurdities and nonsense: "Sitting on a cornflake, waiting for the van to come"; an "elementary penguin" reciting Hare Krishna; "semolina pilchards" climbing up the Eiffel Tower. Still, people searched high and low for hidden meanings.

Let It Be

When I find myself in times of trouble,
Mother Mary comes to me

Despite its gospel-inspired melody, there's nothing particularly religious about this famous ballad by Paul. The "times of trouble" allude to real heartbreak in the lives of the Beatles themselves; "Mother Mary" names none other than Paul's own mother, who died when he was 14 years old.

Get Back

Jo Jo was a man who
thought he was a loner,
But he knew it couldn't last

This song began as Paul's sarcastic response to people who professed the opinion that immigrant workers should just "get back to where [they] once belonged"; Paul dropped the idea as politically controversial but retained the refrain, which works on its own. "Get Back" is basic rock 'n' roll, and its appearance signaled a return to the band's roots. Recorded in a one-day studio session, the song went on to sell nearly 5 million copies around the globe.

Charles De Gaulle (1890-1970). French general and statesman, first president of the Fifth Republic (1959-69). Having fled to London as a wartime refugee (1940-44), De Gaulle came to embody the cause of the Resistance against the German occupation of France.

John F. Kennedy (1917-63). President of the United States (1960-63). Elected at age 43, he became the youngest president in U.S. history. He was assassinated on November 22, 1963, in circumstances that are still debated.

Lyndon B. Johnson (1908-73). President of the United States (1963-68). As Kennedy's vice-president, Johnson became president after Kennedy's assassination and was then elected in 1964. He was responsible for the escalation of the war in Vietnam.

Nikita Khrushchev (1894-1971). Soviet Communist leader, premier of the USSR (1958-64). He was responsible for "destalinization."

Fidel Castro (born 1926). Cuban revolutionary and premier of Cuba. He has been in power since 1959.

Ernesto "Che" Guevara (1928-67). Cuban revolutionary and political leader. He left Cuba to foster revolutionary activity abroad and was killed in Bolivia.

Malcolm X (1925-65). African-American militant leader of the civil rights movement. He was assassinated in New York in 1965.

Martin Luther King, Jr. (1929-68). American clergyman and civil rights leader, advocate of nonviolence; awarded the Nobel Peace Prize in 1964. He was assassinated in 1968.

Mao Zedong (1893-1976). Founder of the People's Republic of China and ruler (1949-76). As totalitarian dictator he led his country to world power.

Ho Chi Minh (1890-1969). Vietnamese nationalist leader, president of North Vietnam (1954-69). As head of the Viet-Minh, he fought the Japanese in World War II and then conducted a successful war against French colonial rule. When the United States intervened, he continued the war with support of China and the Soviet Union.

Harold Wilson (1916-95). British statesman, prime minister (1964-70). A member of the Labor party, his name is forever linked to years of British prosperity.

General Francisco Franco (1892-1975). Spanish general and *caudillo* ("leader") of Spain after the military uprising that started the Spanish civil w Under his iron rule, Spain was the only country western Europe without a democratic governmen the 1960s.

Moshe Dayan (1915-81). Israeli military leade Hero of the 1956 war, he waged the Six-Day War i 1967, which resulted in victory for Israel.

Gamal Abdel Nasser (1918-70). President of Eg (1954-70). He nationalized the Suez Canal and soug to federate the Arab world; he led two wars agains Israel, in 1956 and 1967, which Egypt lost.

Jawaharlal Nehru (1889-1964). Indian statesm prime minister of India (1947-64). He was a pioneer the national independence movement. His daughter Indira Gandhi, became prime minister in 1966.

Yasir Arafat (born 1929). Leader of the Pales Liberation Organization (PLO). Under his leaders a series anti-Israeli bombings began in 1967.

Paul VI (Giovanni Battista Montini) (1897-19 Pope, successor of John XXIII in 1963. He oversa the Second Vatican Council (1962-65), convened to renew the church. One of its changes was the permission of vernacularization of the liturgy.

Yuri A. Gagarin (1934-68). Soviet cosmonaut. In 1961 he became first human to orbit the earth.

Neil Armstrong (born 1930). American astronaut. As a crew member aboard the *Apollo XI* flight, he became the first human being to walk on the Moon in 1969.

Aristotle Onassis (1902-75). Greek shipowner and financier. He was once the world's richest man, owner of a fleet with 4.3 million tons of shipping. He married Jacqueline Bouvier Kennedy in 1968.

Maria Callas (1923-77). Greek-American opera singer. Considered the greatest soprano of all time.

Pablo Picasso (1881-1973). Spanish artist considered the foremost figure in twentieth-century art. In 1963, a Picasso museum opened in Barcelona, Spain.

Andy Warhol (1929-87). American artist and filmmaker. A leading proponent of pop art, which revolutionized popular conceptions of art, he is sometimes credited with erasing the distinction between popular and high culture. He is famous for his images of such ordinary items as Coke bottles and soup cans.

Brigitte Bardot (born 1934). French actress.

After the death of Marilyn Monroe, Bardot became the world's most famous sex symbol and movie star.

Elizabeth Taylor (born 1932). American actress. She and her husband Richard Burton were a world-famous Hollywood couple.

Alfred Hitchcock (1899-1979). English-American filmmaker. During the 1960s, the "Master of Suspense" created two of the most memorable thrillers, *The Birds* and *Psycho*.

Peter Sellers (1925-80). British actor. His disarming clumsiness and false French accent in his role as inspector Clouseau, hero of *The Pink Panther* and sequels, had audiences in stitches. The Beatles adored him.

Alain Delon (born 1935). French actor. He gave a triumphant performance alongside Claudia Cardinale in *Rocco and His Brothers* and Luchino Visconti's *The Leopard*.

Jean-Luc Godard (born 1930). French filmmaker. From *Breathless* to *Pierrot le Fou*, he was the Picasso of French cinema's New Wave.

François Truffaut (1932-84). French filmmaker. With *Jules et Jim*, he brought worldwide attention to cinema's New Wave.

Ingmar Bergman (born 1917). Swedish filmmaker. Known for his startlingly vivid examinations of personal torment and existential angst.

Luis Buñuel (1900-78). Spanish filmmaker. His many provocative and sarcastic films included *Viridiana* and *Belle de Jour*, which attacked the hypocrisy of European society.

Herbert von Karajan (born 1908). Austrian orchestra conductor. His recordings of Beethoven symphonies earned him worldwide acclaim.

Yehudi Menuhin (born 1916). American violinist. He has introduced little-known works and promoted music worldwide.

Christiaan Barnard (born 1923). South African surgeon. In December 1967 he performed the first human heart transplant.

Jim Clark (died 1968). British auto racer. By the time of his death in a racing accident, he had racked up a total of 25 Grand Prix victories.

Jean-Claude Killy (born 1943). French skier and gold medal winner in the 1968 Olympics.

Pelé (born 1940). Brazilian soccer star and two-time winner of the World Cup (1958, 1970).

1969: YESTERDAY

One great dream of the 1960s, the conquest of outer space, is realized in a spectacular triumph on July 21, 1969, when the *Apollo XI*'s Lunar Module lands on the Sea of Tranquility and Astronaut Neil Armstrong becomes the first human to set foot on the Moon. Back on Earth, the atmosphere is less than euphoric. Skeptics wonder why the huge expenditures on the space program aren't being put to better use relieving the suffering of people on the planet. And to be sure, the year 1969 is not without its tragic headlines, the worst being a famine in Biafra, a central African nation that has broken off from Nigeria. For the first time in history

television news cameras are there to broadcast wrenching images of starving black children with skeletal frames and grotesquely distended stomachs, some so weak they are unable to lift themselves off the ground. Meanwhile, in Vietnam, the American army has lost more than 30,000 men since its intervention began and continues its regular bombardment of Viet-Minh positions. A growing number of American students, horrified by their country's use of napalm against innocent Vietnamese citizens, begins demonstrations on campuses and in Washington, D.C. In the Middle East, tensions are running high in the aftermath of the Six-Day War of

June 1967, in which Egypt's entire air force was wiped out by the Israeli army. Palestinian groups, supported by Egypt, Jordan, and Syria, retaliate with acts of terrorism.

In Northern Ireland (Ulster), riots break out between Catholics and Protestants in Belfast in the summer of 1969; one series of violent outbreaks leaves eight dead and some 500 wounded across the country. For the first time, the British armed forces fire on Catholic protesters. A new generation of youths, increasingly restless and increasingly aware of their own power, begins to do whatever they can to change the world. Society tells them to grow up, do their school

CAME SUDDENLY

work, find a job, get married, and settle down—but what, they ask, is the point? Given what is happening in the world, the values of their parents seem to make little sense. In France, a student revolt of unprecedented scale takes place in May 1968, shaking the entire country to its foundations and triggering a general strike that paralyzes the nation for an entire month. The adults have no choice but to pay attention to their children's dreams and also to their protests.

In the United States, in 1968, the Reverend Martin Luther King, Jr., is struck down by an assassin's bullet; when Dr. King falls, the last reason against violent confrontation for civil rights seems to fall with him. Black civil rights activists soon join in impassioned demonstrations against the scourge of racism in America—or anywhere. At the Olympic Games in Mexico that year, the black American athletes Tommie Smith and John Carlos symbolically raise their fists while on the podium receiving their medals. Meanwhile, the radical Black Panthers are calling for violent retribution by black people against the white police officers who have repressed them for so long.

Even the dream of "peace and love" seems to be ending. The famous Woodstock rock festival—450,000 people camped outside listening peacefully to four days of American and British rock bands—takes place in August 1969; in December of the same year, violence erupts at a Rolling Stones concert in Altamount, California, when members of the Hell's Angels motorcycle gang riot and kill a member of the audience: to some people, the event signals the demise of rock.

But by then, the 1960s seem to be over for good: the years have run out, and so have the good times. As John will sing in 1970, "the dream is over." The people intent on changing society are no longer saying it with flowers, but with guns.

concerts in small places along the way. The band Wings is born and goes on to colossal success in the 1970s, appealing especially to younger fans. The music of Paul McCartney and Wings is consistently lighthearted and unpretentious, ideal for dancing and good times. Some "serious" critics deride Paul's music as mere fluff, and its charming simplicity makes it hard for some people to take it seriously as "art." But it is unmistakably Paul, and his natural talent, persistent hard work, and historic influence on popular music will always be undeniable. He has never stopped making music, with some 20 albums to his credit over a span of two decades. In the 1980s, after Wings, he begins a series of collaborations with other artists, notably Stevie Wonder and Michael Jackson. While on a memorable world tour in 1990, in which he attracts a crowd of nearly 200,000 on a single night in Rio de Janeiro, he plays all of his most famous Beatles songs, from "Can't Buy Me Love" to "Let It Be."

Paul

After Brian Epstein's death in 1967, Paul wants to assume control of the Beatles. The documentary film *Let It Be* reveals the failure of his attempt. In 1970, he makes the final break and starts his life over from scratch. For Paul, there is only one way: music. With his wife, Linda, and several musician friends, he takes off on a road trip around England, giving impromptu

PAUL AND JOHN

John

John Lennon's relationship with Yoko Ono begins in 1968. We have her to thank for the transformation of "John the Beatle" into John Lennon the individual. Everything about Yoko is new and experimental, from the recordings of odd noises to the political statements using mass media, like her "love-in" (in which the couple spend several days in bed) for peace. She encourages John to try Arthur Janov's "primal scream therapy." Acting as both mother and mentor, Yoko inspires John's wrenching confessional album, *Plastic Ono Band*, released in early 1971, shortly after *Imagine*. For the first time, John addresses public issues in his music, sending political as well as philosophical and spiritual "messages."

Following several records and political actions in New York, Lennon returns to his sources with the album *Rock 'n' Roll*, taking up again some of the beloved songs of his youth. After a difficult period that includes a temporary separation from Yoko, Lennon abandons music to become a "house husband," devoting himself to the care of his son Sean and leading the life of a recluse. Finally, in 1980, he breaks a long silence with *Double Fantasy*, his first record with Yoko since 1972. The main track, "(Just

Like) Starting Over," is laden with personal meaning.

On December 8, 1980, a "nowhere man" jumps out of the shadows in front of the Dakota, John and Yoko's Manhattan apartment building, and shoots John dead as Yoko stands by in horror. The night before, Lennon had stopped to give his future assassin an autograph.

LIFE GOES ON:

In 1968, George encounters the Indian sitar master Ravi Shankar and soon becomes passionately committed to learning the art of "transcendental meditation" under the tutelage of the Maharishi Mahesh Yogi. Of the four Beatles he is the most ready for the relief of separation; he is, in fact, the first to experience great success in a solo career, with his 1970 hit single "My Sweet Lord." His triple-album *All Things Must Pass* follows soon after. In 1971, Harrison helps organize a mega-concert featuring Bob Dylan, Eric Clapton, and Ravi Shankar for the relief of Bangladeshi children—an innovation that spawns many descendants, including the "Live Aid" benefit for starving Ethiopians in 1985.

In the mid-1970s, George suffers a long dry spell and even considers quitting music altogether. He turns to producing films, starting with *Time Bandits*. In 1988, he makes a big musical comeback with "Got My Mind Set on You," his first hit in a long while. He later forms a "supergroup" called the Traveling Wilburys, with Bob Dylan, Roy Orbison, Jeff Lynne, and Tom Petty. Since 1978, he has lived in an English country manor house with his second wife, Olivia, and their children.

George

George is apparently the first to want out of the group. On August 29, 1966, at San Francisco's Candlestick Park, the Beatles give their last live concert. Traveling home to London after the show, in the comfort of the airplane, George utters a sigh of relief: "That's it. I'm not a Beatle anymore."

GEORGE AND RINGO

Ringo

Of the four Beatles, Ringo has always had the hardest time gaining acceptance as a serious musical artist in his own right. Perhaps this is why most people have a soft spot in their heart for him. He's the only Beatle to succeed in getting his former colleagues back together to help on solo records. After a brief career as an actor in 1968, he seeks the diversion of recording two albums of American traditional songs. Ringo enjoys great success with his solo career until the mid-1970s. A string of significant setbacks follow, in both his career and his health. In 1981 he marries his second wife, actress Barbara Bach, but by then he has sunk into alcohol abuse, and he disappears from sight, not to resurface for almost the entire decade. He is fortunate to have many good friends, including George Harrison, Bob Dylan, and Jeff Lynne, to lean on during the hard times ("I'll get by with a little help from my friends" proves true).

In the early 1990s, Ringo mounts a comeback with his "All-Starr Band." Meanwhile, his son, Zak, is a musician on the California rock scene.

1. The Beatles first 45-r.p.m. record was:

  a) *"Please Please Me"*   b) *"Love Me Do"*   c) *"My Bonnie"*

2. Who was the first Beatle to record a solo album?

  a) *Ringo Starr*   b) *John Lennon*   c) *George Harrison*

3. A rumor circulated in 1969 that one of the Beatles had died. Which one?

a) *John Lennon*   b) *Paul McCartney*   c) *Ringo Starr*

4. What is the total running time of "Hey Jude"?

a) *5'45"*   b) *6'55"*   c) *7'15"*

5. What was the last album recorded by the Beatles?

a) *Abbey Road*   b) *Let It Be*   c) *Yellow Submarine (film soundtrack)*

6. When did the Beatles perform their last public concert?

a) *August 29, 1966*   b) *June 25, 1967*   c) *January 30, 1969*

7. What Beatles song has been performed the most by other artists?

a) *"Hey Jude"*   b) *"Yesterday"*   c) *"Something"*

8. How many albums (not counting compilations) did the Beatles release in the United States during their time together, through 1970, the year of their separation?

a) *15*   b) *17*   c) *21*

9. In what year was the Apple record label launched?

a) *1967*   b) *1968*   c) *1969*

10. What was the best-selling 45-r.p.m. record in the United States during the 1960s?

  a) *"I Want To Hold Your Hand" by the Beatles*   b) *"It's Now Or Never" by Elvis Presley*   c) *"Hey Jude" by the Beatles*

11. How many songs by George Harrison did the Beatles release?

  a) *23*   b) *17*   c) *20*

12. Match each Beatle to his mate:

  a) *Maureen and*   b) *Jane and*   c) *Cynthia and*   d) *Patti and*

TEST YOUR BEATLES KNOWLEDGE

1. *b.* Released in England by Parlophone on October 5, 1962, "Love Me Do" never went higher than number 17 on the New Musical Express hit list; but when it came out in the United States on April 27, 1964, it made it to number one for a week on the American pop charts. "Please Please Me" was released in England on January 11, 1963, and soon topped the charts there. "My Bonnie" was actually the band's first recording, but not as the Beatles. This song, first released in Germany in June 1961, was credited to Tony Sheridan and the Beat Brothers.

2. *c.* George Harrison was first out of the gates with his Wonderwall Music album, released in England on November 1, 1968. Recorded partly in Bombay with Indian musicians, this recording of original instrumental music contained the psychedelic film Wonderwall, made by Joe Musson, a friend of Harrison's, with Jane Birkin.

3. *b.* At the end of 1969, a disc jockey at a radio station in Detroit, Michigan, spread the rumor that Paul McCartney had been killed in a car accident three years earlier and replaced by an impostor (in seclusion on his farm, Paul was, in fact, temporarily out of sight). As proof, the DJ pointed to details on the cover of the just released Abbey Road album, which presented the four Beatles walking across a street. According to the DJ, this was instead Paul's funeral procession. John was the minister (dressed in a suit); George (in jeans) was the undertaker; Ringo was the gravedigger; and barefoot Paul was the corpse (it helped that the left-handed Paul was presented holding a cigarette in his right hand). Other signs of Paul's "death" soon turned up on the covers of other albums and in the lyrics of songs.

4. *c.* This single, released on August 26, 1968, was both the Beatles' longest and their most popular. It was recorded with an orchestra of forty musicians.

5. *a.* While it is true that Let It Be was the last Beatles album to be officially released, in May 1970, it had been recorded in the early months of 1969, only to have temporarily shelved. The Beatles got back together for the last time in the early summer of 1969 to record Abbey Road, which came out that September.

6. *c.* The last public performance by the Beatles was given atop the Apple building, at 3 Savile Row in London—an impromptu, open-air show for the documentary film Let It Be. Their last official concert tour ended in America on August 29, 1966, at San Francisco's Candlestick Park. On June 25, 1967, the Beatles sang "All You Need Is Love" in a live television show broadcast via satellite from London.

7. *b.* The different versions of "Yesterday" by other artists number in the hundreds (the best known is Ray Charles's 1967 recording); in fact, the Guinness Book of Records makes it the most "covered" song in history. "Hey Jude" was redone by Wilson Pickett in 1969; Shirley Bassey and Frank Sinatra both did their own interpretations of "Something."

8. *c.* Here is the list of releases in the U.S.A.: Meet the Beatles! (1964); Introducing . . . the Beatles (1964); The Beatles (1964); Introducing New (1964); A Hard Day's Night (1964); Something New (1964); The Beatles' Story (1964); Beatles '65 (1965); The Beatles' Second Album (1964); Beatles VI (1965); Help! (1965); Rubber Soul (1965); "Yesterday" . . . and Today (1966); Revolver (1966); Sgt. Pepper's Lonely Hearts Club Band (1967); Magical Mystery Tour (1967); The Beatles (1968); Yellow Submarine (1969); Abbey Road (1969); Hey Jude (1970); Let it Be (1970).

9. *b.* The release of the "Hey Jude" single in August 1968 marked the label's official debut: another 45-r.p.m. "Those Were the Days," by a Welsh singer named Mary Hopkin, was also released by Apple in its first month.

10. *c.* "I Want To Hold Your Hand" lasted seven weeks at the top of the American charts, selling over 5 million copies; but "Hey Jude" topped the charts for nine straight weeks and is the group's biggest-selling American hit.

11. *c.* The Beatles began recording Harrison's songs in 1965. Among them are "If I Needed Someone"; "Taxman"; "While My Guitar Gently Weeps"; "Here Comes the Sun"; "Within You Without You"; and "I Me Mine." "Something," released in 1969, was the only song by Harrison ever released on the A-side of a 45-r.p.m. single.

12. *a:* Ringo. Maureen Cox was a hairdresser's assistant in Liverpool who frequented the Cavern Club. She and Ringo were married in 1965 and had three children together: Zak, Jason, and Lee. The couple was divorced in 1975. Ringo remarried in 1981, to actress Barbara Bach.
b: Paul. Jane Asher came from a respectable London family and had been a television, movie, and stage actress since childhood. They were engaged in 1967 but broke it off the next year. Paul married the American photographer Linda Eastman in 1969.
c: John. Cynthia Powell was a student at the Liverpool Art School. She and John met Yoko. They separated in 1968 after John met Yoko. 1963. They were married in Liverpool in 1963. John and Cynthia were divorced in 1968.
d: George. Patti Boyd and George were married in 1966 and divorced in 1977. In 1978 George married Olivia Arias.

91

AND IN THE END:

"No Elvis, Beatles, or the Rolling Stones!" proclaims the Clash, pioneers of punk rock, in 1977. This is a dramatic way of saying the time has come to forget the Golden Age of sixties rock and move on to a new era. But admitting that the dream is over proves painful. There are persistent rumors throughout the 1970s that the Beatles are going to make a comeback. In 1976 a concert promoter offers them $30 million for a single concert. They refuse. Some people seem to believe that John, Paul, George, and Ringo possess some magical force to bring back the enthusiasm and optimism of the 1960s. In 1973, two double albums, *1962-1966* and *1967-1970*, bring together the band's greatest hits, setting off the first wave of Beatles nostalgia. Since then, not a year has passed without some commemoration of the band. In the 1970s a musical comedy and TV series on British television, "The Rutles," by the Monty Python group, celebrates the memory of the band through gentle parody. The Beatles albums themselves are constantly being rereleased and have never ceased to sell. Even the singles have held their own, especially "Love Me Do" and "Let It Be." In 1987, on the occasion of the rerelease of all the Beatles albums on compact disk, *Sergeant Pepper* jumps to the top of the British charts—two decades after its original release. In 1991, the American record industry announces that *Abbey Road* has sold 9 million copies since its release, with *The Beatles* close behind at about 7 million copies sold. In 1995 the announcement of a new double album,

THE BEATLES' MUSICAL LONGEVITY

the first volume of a major new Beatles release entitled *Anthology*, shows that the popularity of the Beatles has not waned. To mark the occasion, Paul, George, and Ringo gather in a recording studio for the first time in 25 years and add tracks to two songs left unfinished by John at the time of his death. The legacy of the Beatles is still far from exhausted. Their music will remain an unsurpassable point of reference for all bands in years to come. In the 1970s, Supertramp and the Electric Light Orchestra (ELO) draw heavily on the Beatles' orchestral innovations. Elton John is greatly inspired by the Beatles' interpretation of the American rhythm and blues tradition. Later, artists of the New Wave, such as Blondie and Elvis Costello, emulate the energy and melodic freshness of the early Beatles. And in the 1980s, the careers of groups like U2 are reminiscent of the adventurousness and constant evolution of the Beatles. From megastars like Prince to lesser-known rockers in America and Britain, just about every rock musician at one point or another pays homage to the Beatles.

The Beatles have become larger-than-life figures, and their music virtually defines "classic rock." Contemporary musicians draw on the literature of the Beatles as if it were traditional folklore handed down from time immemorial. Like a musical garden tended by all humanity, the music of the Beatles continues to bear fruit season after season.

IMAGINE: THE FUTURE

In the 1960s, people were brimming with enthusiasm as they imagined a future of high-speed commuter trains or monorails speeding from city to city. Someday soon, it seemed, a family might be able to board its own small spaceship and go off for an afternoon on Mars. Tiny food pills would satisfy all nutritional needs. Even death would be overcome: the bodies of the dead would be frozen in special caskets using the revolutionary technology of cryogenics and then "thawed" and revived when medical science conquered the disease in question. Walt Disney, known for his zeal for futuristic science, was rumored to have taken elaborate measures to ensure that his body would be thus preserved, in a modern version of *Sleeping Beauty*. The rapid pace of technological progress made the future a source of endless fascination. But modern technology created reasons for anxiety as well as the stuff of dreams: the 1960s were also a decade of the arms race and the cold war. Air raid drills were a common feature in schools all across America; everyone knew that there were more than enough missiles in silos and aboard nuclear submarines to destroy not just all the world's cities, but human civilization itself. In this atmosphere, spies took on leading roles, and thus alongside the Beatles the character of James Bond stands as an icon of the period. Outfitted with a host of sophisticated gadgets, such as a radio transmitter mounted in the heel of his shoe (a devise that seemed extremely advanced at the time, before the arrival of today's miniature cellular phones), Agent 007 was in constant struggle against equally high-tech adversaries. The leaders of the ultra-evil organization known as S.P.E.C.T.R.E., with their soulless agents and futuristic devices, waged all-out war against the civilized world. Audiences of the blockbuster Bond movies saw the arms race and the cold war acted out in exciting, elaborate dramas in which the good guys triumphed over the forces of evil. Looking back on the sixties today, some people recall James Bond more fondly than they do the Beatles. The Beatles were the clearest expression of the counterculture revolution of that period, and there are those who blame some of today's ills on that revolution. Whereas the evil forces that Bond outwitted seem to have been defeated (at least temporarily), the forces against which the Beatles sang their songs—selfish materialism, prejudice, religious bigotry, violence, loneliness—have yet to be overcome. The problems are still with us, but so too is the music of the Beatles, and the true meaning of the words has never changed.

INDEX

BOOKS FOR FURTHER READING

Brown, Peter H., and Steven Gaines. *The Love You Make: An Insider's Story of the Beatles*. New York: NAL Penguin, 1984.
Giuliano, Geoffrey. *Blackbird: The Life and Times of Paul McCartney*. New York: NAL Penguin, 1992.
———. *Dark Horse: The Secret Life of George Harrison*. New York: NAL Penguin, 1991.
Glassman, Bruce. *Lennon and McCartney: Their Magic and Their Music*. Woodbridge, Ct.: Blackbirch, 1995.
Lennon, John. *In His Own Write and A Spaniard in the Works*. New York: NAL Penguin, 1967.
Lewisohn, Mark. *The Complete Beatles Chronicle*. New York: Crown, 1992.
Loewen, N. *The Beatles*. Vero Beach, Fl.: Rourke, 1989.
Neises, Charles P. *The Beatles Reader: A Selection of Contemporary Views, News, and Reviews of the Beatles in Their Heyday*. Ann Arbor, Mich.: Popular Culture Ink., 1991.
Norman, Philip. *Shout! The Beatles in Their Generation*. New York: Elm Tree, 1982.
Taylor, Derek. *It Was Twenty Years Ago Today*. New York: Bantam, 1987.

ILLUSTRATIONS

PHOTOGRAPHS

PHOTO CREDITS

TEXT CREDITS